WHY WASTE FOOD?

FOOD CONTROVERSIES

SERIES EDITOR: ANDREW F. SMITH

Everybody eats. Yet few understand the importance of food
in our lives and the decisions we make each time we eat.
The Food Controversies series probes problems created by
the industrial food system and examines proposed alternatives.

Already published:

Fast Food: The Good, the Bad and the Hungry Andrew F. Smith
Food Adulteration and Food Fraud Jonathan Rees
What's So Controversial about Genetically Modified Food? John T. Lang
What's the Matter with Meat? Katy Keiffer

WHY WASTE FOOD?

ANDREW F. SMITH

REAKTION BOOKS

Published by Reaktion Books Ltd
Unit 32, Waterside
44–48 Wharf Road
London N1 7UX, UK

www.reaktionbooks.co.uk

First published 2020
Copyright © Andrew F. Smith 2020

Printed and bound in Great Britain
by TJ International, Padstow, Cornwall

A catalogue record for this book is available from the British Library
ISBN 978 1 78914 344 7

CONTENTS

PROLOGUE

No one argues for wasting food, since it is not in anyone's self-interest to do so. Farmers lose money growing crops that they cannot sell. Food processors pay for the disposal of production waste, manufacturing errors and food recalls. Wholesalers and retailers lose money on food and food products discarded owing to expired freshness dates, spoilage, overstocking and customer returns – and then they have to pay for the disposal of those items. Restaurateurs lose money on buying food that is not sold, and then they have to pay for the removal of food their customers leave behind on their plates. Ultimately, we consumers pay the costs for all 'upstream' losses and waste – and then we waste even more by buying food that we eventually throw into the bin.

Wasting food is not in our collective self-interest either for it is a major contributor to global warming. It accounts for about 8 per cent of the world's total greenhouse gas emissions (GHGs). This figure doesn't include the GHGs and other environmental issues associated with the use of water, fertilizer, pesticides and fuel needed to produce and transport food that is discarded. And then there is the indirect environmental damage caused by food and beverage packaging, cartons, wrappers, cans, plastic bags, straws, cups, utensils and plastic bottles that end up in dumps or as litter on streets, roadways and beaches, and in waterways and oceans.

Finally, there are the ethical issues against wasting food while hundreds of millions of people suffer from hunger, malnutrition or food insecurity throughout the world and often in our own neighbourhoods. There are, of course, many reasons for global hunger, but an actual food shortage is not one today. Enough food is produced to adequately feed everyone in the world, with plenty left over. If food that ends up as waste could be equitably distributed to those in need, global hunger and malnutrition could be eliminated.

Yet despite financial, environmental and ethical reasons to not waste food, about one-third (1.4 billion tons) of all food grown for human consumption is lost or discarded every year. Globally, this works out to about a trillion dollars of economic losses – or about 1.5 per cent of the total worldwide economy. As enormous as these figures are, they do not include food crops grown for other uses, such as ethanol production, pet food or animal feed. Neither do these figures include the massive amount of edible (but unpopular and unsaleable) seafood netted by commercial fishing industries and then dumped overboard. And neither do these figures include the overconsumption of vast quantities of food by many people, particularly in well-to-do countries, that has resulted in the global obesity crisis.

If wasting food is such an undeniable negative, why do we discard so much? Despite all the global clamour surrounding the topic, many people remain unaware of the harm that food waste needlessly causes, and many who are aware just don't see reducing or eliminating food waste as a priority in their lives. Businesses find it easier and less risky to simply dump excess food than try to find ways to prevent waste or figure out what to do with food that has become inedible. It makes no sense for farmers to harvest excess food that they cannot sell, and it is far easier for many processors, retailers, restaurateurs and homemakers to toss unwanted food into the bin than it is to figure out how to reuse, recover or recycle it.

What makes this an even more significant matter is that the United Nations projects the world population to increase to 9.7 billion by 2050 – just three decades away – while global warming will decrease food production significantly in many areas of the world. Conservative projections conclude that global food production will need to increase by 25 to 70 per cent by 2050 to meet population growth and agricultural losses due to global warming. One obvious solution is to reduce food waste, which would not require putting more land under cultivation – and would not require the use of more water, energy, fertilizer and pesticides. The good news is that thousands of governmental projects and programmes, non-profit organizations, foundations, social enterprises, start-ups and for-profit businesses around the world are doing just that.

The term 'food waste' is variously defined. *Why Waste Food?* focuses on food that is grown or raised for human consumption that is removed from the food system, such as via incineration or dumping into landfill, waterways or oceans. It examines causes of avoidable food waste and highlights programmes and businesses underway around the world to feed people, save the planet and make money – all using food that is frequently discarded.

Food waste is not a new phenomenon: it has been an on-and-off topic of public interest for more than a century, but only during the past few decades has reducing and preventing food waste emerged as a sustained global priority. Chapter One targets the question: why is food waste now a major global concern?

Food waste begins on farms. Chapter Two looks at the types of edible food, particularly fruits and vegetables, that never make it to market. Farmers who specialize in growing fruit and vegetables sign contracts with retailers to deliver crops that meet the buyers' standards. When crops do not meet these standards, the buyer rejects them – and farmers end up with an excess of perfectly edible produce. This chapter looks at the programmes intended to reduce farmed waste, such as gleaning and changing supermarket policies. It also looks at the businesses that have emerged to convert what was once wasted on farms to saleable goods. Finally, it examines issues associated with food transportation and storage.

The third chapter examines the waste caused by commercial food processing. Historically, edible by-products from food production were given to local farmers for feeding livestock or composting, but today a large percentage ends up in landfill. This chapter also explores why confusing date labels printed on packages by manufacturers create waste downstream in the food system. Solutions to this include improved planning and internal control systems. In addition, many processors have made arrangements with start-ups to 'upcycle' manufacturing waste into other saleable products, such as foods, drinks, biofuel, furniture, clothes and compostable plates.

The fourth chapter looks at how supermarkets and other food retailers generate unprecedented amounts of waste, and examines responses to their waste, such as dumpster diving and collecting surplus edible food for delivery to anti-hunger programmes. Supermarket waste has become the subject of films and television programmes, which have encouraged large chains to reduce waste and challenged them to demonstrate how they will make greater reductions in the future. Innovations such as zero-waste shops and 'anti-supermarkets' sell or distribute food that the big shops discard and several countries have mandated an end to supermarket waste altogether.

Restaurateurs and other food-service operators project how much food they will need, and order accordingly. If they order too little, they run out of supplies and lose sales; if they order too much, excesses are often discarded. Additional waste is caused by bad planning; kitchen staff throwing out scraps and leftovers rather than figuring out how to use them in other dishes; and the vast amount of plate waste produced by customers. Issues and solutions related to food-service waste, including a plethora of new apps and 'zero-waste restaurants', are examined in Chapter Five.

All evidence points to consumers and consumer-facing businesses as major contributors to food waste in high-income countries. Food is wasted by homemakers who buy too much due to lack of planning, or throw out leftovers rather than trying to reuse them, or discard edible food that has neared or passed its freshness date. Websites, apps, cookbooks and smart kitchen devices offer waste-reducing techniques of menu planning, shopping and preparation; these and other solutions are discussed in Chapter Six.

Most foods and beverages are sold in packages, such as bottles, cans, boxes and bags, that are meant to keep the product fresh, thereby avoiding waste. However, food packaging is also a major source of rubbish that ends up in landfill or oceans. Plastic containers, bags, bottles, cups and other food-related items are key contributors to environmental degradation, particularly oceanic pollution. Chapter Seven looks at the overwhelming quantity of food-related waste and its effects on the environment and health, and examines solutions, such as 'light-weighting', the invention of zero-waste shops, the creation of biodegradable packaging materials and other 'smart' packaging techniques.

The Epilogue re-examines proposed solutions and identifies challenges confronting food-waste reduction efforts.

1
WAR ON FOOD WASTE

Conserving food and preventing its waste have been crucial matters confronting humankind for millennia. Failure to store or preserve food in times of plenty could result in hunger, famine and death in times of want. Virtually every religion forbade wasting food, and saving food was a value built into the culture of most communities. Farmers carefully stored crops and preserved food for later use, and they plowed under what was unharvested or leftover for fertilizer. Likewise, family culinary traditions passed down from mother to daughter stressed the importance of wasting nothing and finding uses for every bit of edible food. Vegetable peels, bones and less desirable animal products were used to make stocks and soups. Excess scraps were often fed to livestock. Roots, leaves, feathers, bones, fish scales and tails and spoiled food were composted for use as fertilizer. These techniques worked well in rural regions, but as people around the world moved from rural to urban areas, the amount of food waste exploded.

During the twentieth century, public concerns about wasted food surfaced in periods of shortages and rationing, such as during the First and Second World Wars. Nations affected by war conducted massive propaganda campaigns to encourage citizens not to waste food, which was desperately needed for the war effort. Food waste was declared a 'sin', while conserving food was a patriotic duty. Slogans like 'Waste Not, Want Not' and 'Don't Waste Food While Others Starve!' were popularized during war years and posters, flyers, pamphlets and radio spots encouraging conservation promised that 'Food Will Win the War'. When the wars were over and agricultural production surged, however, the anti-food-waste campaigns ended and public concern with saving food dwindled.

Declining Food Prices = Increasing Waste

Throughout the last century, mechanization increased yields on farms; improved transportation systems permitted easier access from farms to retailers; and the rise of supermarkets, with their high-volume purchasing, passed on savings to shoppers. Even as food prices were dropping, wages were rising for many people. The result of lower food costs and higher pay was that families spent smaller proportions of their income on buying food. In 1900, urban u.s. households spent an estimated 42.5 per cent of their take-home pay on food. By the twenty-first century, this had shrunk to about 6.6 per cent for food prepared and consumed at home. Similar patterns were seen in other industrialized countries: by the twenty-first century, uk households expended about 8.2 per cent of their income on food, while French and South Korean households spent about 13.5 per cent.[1]

Lower prices diminished the value of food throughout production and consumption systems in industrialized countries. Farmers earned less for their crops, so they maximized production in order to maintain income or generate greater profits. This resulted in massive overproduction of food, which has been – and continues to be – a major contributor to the staggering increases in levels of food waste. Growers intentionally produced excess crops to meet exacting contracts with retailers, and then ploughed under any unsold produce. For food processors, lower prices made it more practical to dispose of leftover ingredients than to devise ways to use them. For supermarket managers, it was easier to overstock shelves to meet consumer expectations, and then toss out food and food products that had passed their prime. Rather than worry about off-flavours, funky odours or risk potential food poisoning, retailers and consumers readily discarded potentially questionable items.

Decreasing food prices and busy lifestyles also meant that people spent less time shopping for and preparing food – it was easier and more convenient to buy food that was already prepared or just have it delivered. Homemakers were more likely to forget (or ignore) uneaten food in the fridge or pantry until it was spoiled or was no longer appealing. Greater variety made it 'more challenging to control waste and plan ahead'.[2] Consumers did purchase economical, easy-to-prepare mixes, heat-and-eat frozen meals and microwaveable entrées. These changes resulted in the loss of traditional cooking skills once handed down through generations, and thrifty use of food declined as a hallmark of a good home cook.

Low food prices also meant that many consumers ate out more often. Restaurants, cafeterias, commissaries, buffets,

snack bars, lunch counters, kiosks, coffee shops, takeaway
operations and mega fast-food chains thrived. By the early
twenty-first century, consumers in some well-to-do countries
expended almost half of their food budgets on food prepared
outside the home. Leftovers from these meals are typically
tossed out.

Food packaging, such as tin cans, cardboard boxes and
foil wrappings, prolonged the useful life of many foods and
enabled products to be transported more safely over longer
distances from farm to factory to retailer to consumer.
Improved packaging, such as plastic tubs, shrink wrap
and aseptic containers, further extended storage time,
eventually permitting food to be kept in warehouses or
homes for months or even years without degrading. But food
packaging was rarely reusable and most packaging added to
waste streams.

Packaging often meant that retailers and consumers
could not see, smell or touch the contents within the
container, and it was not until containers were open that
consumers found their food had spoiled. To help people
determine whether packaged products were still fresh
and wholesome, processors began labelling foods and
beverages with dates indicating when the product had been
packed, or when its recommended shelf life would expire.
With 'sell-by' or 'best if used by' dates clearly marked,
retailers (and consumers) could discard packaged foods
after the expiration date. But there was no consistency in
the labelling: food companies employed various labelling
systems and terminology. By the 1970s, a confusing array
of fifty different product-dating systems confronted

retailers and consumers, who soon championed the slogan, 'When in doubt, throw it out.'

Waste also increased due to supermarket policies regarding fresh fruit and vegetables. During the second half of the twentieth century, supermarket chains developed stringent standards for produce. Fruit and vegetables had to be well shaped, uniformly sized and attractively coloured, among other specifications. Produce brokers contracted with supermarkets to deliver products that met these standards; fruit and vegetables that did not measure up were rejected. It didn't pay for farmers to harvest produce they couldn't sell, so the excess was often ploughed under, given to animals or dumped at the end of the season.

Landfilling Food Waste

Materials deemed valueless by societies were historically dumped outside town or city limits, often into nearby lakes, rivers or swamps. Coastal cities shipped waste offshore and dumped it into the ocean. As urban areas expanded, new solutions were required to handle the growing volume of waste. Some was burned in bonfires or incinerators. The first 'modern' sanitary landfill was created in Fresno, California, in 1935. There, garbage was compacted and covered daily with soil to reduce odours and limit rodent and insect infestation. Landfills began eating up acreage around many communities throughout the world.

Archaeologists were the first to research waste dumps as a means of understanding a community's daily life at different historical periods. Beginning in 1973 William Rathje, an

American archaeologist, began excavating landfills around Tucson, Arizona. For the next several decades he and his colleagues examined trends in what materials ended up as rubbish. Rathje's and subsequent studies of other sites concluded that food was the single largest component of solid waste in landfills. These studies, however, addressed only a portion of the total food wasted. They did not include food scraps ground up in garbage disposals and washed into sewers or the food waste that was incinerated. Neither did they include food-packaging materials, nor food scraps that ended up as compost or animal fodder.

Precisely how much total food was wasted remained unclear, but a 1980 study in the United Kingdom estimated that 3,100 calories of food were available daily to each resident. As the average person required only 2,300 calories, the authors concluded that a large portion of the remainder was wasted 'in the home as well as in catering establishments and during the storage, distribution and processing of food'.[3] The Economic Research Service of the u.s. Department of Agriculture calculated that the American food system produced 4,200 calories per person per day, which meant that a large portion of the food produced for human consumption was lost or wasted, and much of it ended up in landfill.[4]

Save the Planet

Environmental activists who emerged during the 1960s were concerned with a wide range of issues, including waste disposal. They advocated recycling, reducing and reusing 'waste' rather than dumping it into ever-expanding landfill sites or incinerating it. At their urging, many communities established collection and recycling programmes for specific items, such as paper products, bottles, metal, cans and glass – but not food.

In recycling programmes, the presence of food particles, grease and oil on paper would-be recyclables, such as soiled pizza boxes or grease-stained paper products, could contaminate entire loads of recyclables, making them unusable or greatly reducing their value. In addition, food residue can create unsafe conditions for workers in recycling facilities. Estimates vary, but in the u.s. alone an estimated 25 per cent of paper recyclables are covered primarily with food waste.

Another serious environmental problem emerged with food waste sent to landfill. When food and other organic matter end up in landfills, they are compressed tightly underground and are deprived of oxygen. This results in the production of vast quantities of methane, which is 25 times more damaging to Earth's atmosphere than CO_2. The u.s. Environmental Protection Agency estimated that 63 million tons of food was sent to landfills each year, producing about 34 per cent of all American methane emissions.[5] Studies have demonstrated that food waste is the third largest emitter of greenhouse gases (GHGs). Environmental efforts around the world jumped on the anti-food-waste bandwagon in the hopes of stemming global warming.

As food waste became an important topic within environmental circles, various waste-reduction programmes were proposed. Food recovery hierarchies, for instance, prioritized actions that could prevent or divert wasted food. The best solution, according to most hierarchies, was to reduce the volume of surplus food generated; the second was to get excess food to those in need; the third was to use the surplus food for industrial purposes, such as making biogas or compost; and the worst resort was to dispose of food in landfills.

Governmental agencies began to take action to limit the amount of material being dumped into landfills. The Japanese legislature passed the Law for the Promotion of Effective Utilities of Resources (Recycling Law) in 1991, and a decade later passed the Food Recycling Law. These regulations encouraged businesses to create cyclical manufacturing processes that would reduce, reuse or recycle leftovers. The European Union established the Landfill Directive (1991) with the mission of reducing

negative effects on the environment, in particular the pollution of surface water, groundwater, soil and on the global environment, including the greenhouse effect, as well as any resulting risk to human health, from the landfilling of waste, during the whole life-cycle of the landfill.[6]

Alternatives to Landfilling Food Waste

Traditionally, waste was the end result of a linear economy: food and other goods were produced, sold and consumed, and the remains were discarded. During the 1980s the concept of the 'circular economy' was proposed. Circular economy advocates consider food waste as a resource to be used, and not rubbish to be thrown away.

Composting was one traditional way farmers and home-makers dealt with inedible food and organic and animal waste. The resulting fertilizer could be used on their crops or gardens. As countries urbanized, composting became more difficult in cities and it was more convenient for food processors, retailers and consumers to just toss food waste into rubbish bins that would typically be hauled away by city agencies. As environmental and other issues emerged regarding landfill, governmental agencies, non-profit organizations and for-profit businesses began collecting organic waste and converting it into fertilizer to be distributed via public parks or to farmers. As local and national governments passed laws against tossing food waste into landfill, composting machines emerged for businesses – and homeowners – to dehydrate organic waste (about 70 per cent of which is water) and reduce foul aromas, insects and other pests drawn to waste containers awaiting collection. By the end of the twentieth century, composting businesses emerged in many cities around the world, which picked up organic waste and converted it into fertilizer.

New approaches emerged on how to reuse or recycle food waste. One was to convert food waste and other organic material into biogas via anaerobic digestion – the series of processes by which microorganisms break down organic material into methane, which can then be used as a renewable energy source. Beginning in the 1990s Germany took the lead in constructing anaerobic digestion plants, which offered several advantages: food and other organic waste were kept out of landfills and hence had a limited effect on the environment. The resulting biogas could generate electricity, power trucks collecting organic waste, or be fed into local natural gas pipelines for use in homes and businesses. Anaerobic digestion facilities also produced nutrient-rich 'digestate' to be used as a soil conditioner. Despite these positives, low oil prices in the late 1990s made it unclear whether anaerobic digestion programmes were financially viable.

Feed People

During the 1950s many well-to-do countries established social welfare programmes that provided minimum standards of living for citizens. These programmes were intended in part to mitigate problems of food insecurity. The United States did not develop such a system, but during the 1960s media exposés, governmental commissions and high-profile reports drew attention to the problems of hunger and malnutrition. Non-governmental programmes were instituted to feed the hungry, such as food pantries, soup kitchens and food-rescue programmes sponsored by churches, unions and civic organizations. These community programmes provided food directly to those in need.

Food banks – central locations that accept donations from farmers, food processors, supermarkets, restaurants and other food-service operations – were established throughout the U.S. They collected donations mainly from regional supermarket chains and wholesalers, which offered tonnes of mislabelled or damaged packaged foods, overstock, testmarket products, and foods close to their sell-by or use-by dates. These were then sorted and distributed to affiliated food pantries, soup kitchens and other hunger-relief programmes. This system permitted the safe use of millions of tonnes of food that would otherwise have ended up in landfill – and, more important, it provided sustenance to people who were hungry or food-insecure.

In other countries, welfare systems underwent reforms during the late twentieth century that unsheltered many people. Stagnating wages and shrinking social welfare created the need for alternative food delivery systems for those worst hit by food shortage and food poverty. The food-bank model was established in other countries beginning in the 1980s. In September 1985 Les Restaurants du Coeur (Restaurants of the Heart) was established in France by the comedian and actor Michel Gérard Joseph Colucci to distribute food packages and hot meals to people in need. In Italy, the Fondazione Banco Alimentare Onlus was founded in 1989 to retrieve and distribute undamaged and non-expired food items from retailers that would otherwise have been destroyed. Food banks, however, were not common outside the u.s. until the war on food waste began in earnest during the twenty-first century.

Prelude to War

A major vulnerability of industrialized food systems is that they are dependent on cheap oil to fuel farm equipment, power trucks and ships, make fertilizer and operate manufacturing facilities. When the u.s. and other countries considered invading Iraq in 2002 the price of oil edged up, and when the invasion began in March 2003 oil prices skyrocketed. This caused a huge jump in global prices for corn, wheat and soy, which in turn bumped up the cost of grain-fed pork, beef and chicken.

To alleviate the fuel crisis, the U.S. passed the Renewable Fuel Standard Act, which required refiners to blend increasing amounts of ethanol into gasoline. The programme grew out of an effort by lawmakers to reduce the country's reliance on imported oil, prop up struggling corn and soy farmers and rein in rising greenhouse gas emissions. Brazil, the European Union, Canada, China and other nations also subsidized production of ethanol, a renewable biofuel made largely from sugar cane, sorghum, corn, barley and other grains. However, these programmes diverted staple crops from markets, driving up food prices around the world.

The global food system could have overcome rising oil prices had it not been for simultaneous adverse weather conditions in multiple parts of the world. In Australia, two years of drought decimated the wheat crop. Grain production in Ukraine and Russia, much of whose crops had previously been exported, was also curtailed. India likewise faced domestic food shortages; in June 2006 it stopped exporting sugar, wheat and lentils in an effort to stabilize domestic food prices. India subsequently banned exports of rice and Vietnam reduced rice exports.

As food prices soared globally, speculators jumped into commodities markets, buying up grain futures and pushing food prices still higher. Between 2005 and 2007 food prices leapt by 75 per cent. From the spring to the autumn of 2007 many food prices doubled. By May 2007 the world price of wheat hit $200 per tonne; by early September it rose to more than $400 – the highest price ever recorded for wheat. Three months later, world cereal stocks based as a proportion of production were the lowest ever recorded. Russia imposed price controls on milk, eggs, bread and other staples. Venezuela imposed price controls on food. These policies further decreased the availability of food worldwide as farmers stored or, where possible, exported commodities rather than sell them at artificially low prices. *The Economist*'s food-price index was higher in December 2007 than at any time since it was created in 1845 and the magazine proclaimed 'the end of cheap food'.[7]

A simultaneous challenge was the financial meltdown initiated by a slowing U.S. economy, worsened by the mortgage crisis that hit in December 2007. As business and financial institutions fell victim, the result was the Great Recession, the largest global economic downturn since the Great Depression of the 1930s. Worldwide, large corporations and small companies alike collapsed, and millions of workers lost their jobs. Despite rising unemployment and deflationary pressure on prices, global food prices remained high.

In many parts of the world, unstable oil and food prices made it difficult for many people to make a living. An estimated 110 million people were thrown into poverty and 44 million were undernourished. Infant and child mortality surged. During Ramadan, the government of Morocco fixed prices so people could afford to buy bread – assuming they could find any for sale. Consumer groups in Italy staged a one-day pasta strike. Pakistan deployed paramilitary troops to guard trucks carrying wheat and flour. Malaysian leaders made it a crime to export flour and other products without a licence. Food riots and other forms of unrest erupted in thirty countries. The United Nations Secretary-General Ban Ki-moon reported that the threat of hunger and malnutrition was rapidly growing and that millions of the world's most vulnerable people were at risk.

Experts projected that food prices would continue to increase by 5 per cent per year for the next decade.[8] Reports by the United Nations Environment Programme and the World Bank projected that food prices could go up by 30 to 50 per cent within a few decades, forcing those living in extreme poverty to spend up to 90 per cent of their income on food.[9]

In the face of looming crises, scientists, agriculture experts and political leaders organized conferences, academics published articles and books, and foundations and governmental agencies issued reports to help counter ever-rising food prices, growing world hunger and threats to the environment. Some argued for sending more aid to developing countries and improving information systems to monitor and assess the impact of rising food prices. Others proposed bringing new land into cultivation and expanding industrial agriculture – which many environmentalists opposed.

One obvious solution – supported by environmentalists and those concerned with feeding the hungry – was to reduce food waste. The Dutch Ministry of Agriculture, Nature and Food Quality began to focus on food waste in 2006. In Denmark, Selina Juul, a Russian émigré, started a Facebook group in 2008 that became the non-profit organization 'Stop Spild Af Mad' (Stop Wasting Food). She began publishing opinion pieces and articles on food waste in international newspapers, many co-written with prominent politicians; she also collaborated with Danish chefs to publish a cookbook with recipes intended to reduce food waste in the kitchen. Stop Wasting Food quickly became the country's largest consumer movement against food waste. By 2016 these programmes would help Denmark to slash its discarded food by 25 per cent.[10]

France passed the Waste Framework Directive (2008), which defined biowaste as 'biodegradable garden and park waste, food and kitchen waste from households, restaurants, caterers and retail premises, and comparable waste from food-processing plants'. The French Environment and Energy Management Agency funded an anti-food-waste campaign targeting consumers. It included television and radio spots, press adverts and web banners. Consumer surveys were also undertaken to improve understanding of why consumers threw away so much food.

War is Declared

The UK Department for Environment, Food and Rural Affairs (Defra) funded the Waste and Resources Action Programme (WRAP), creating a public–private partnership intended to achieve a circular economy through reducing waste. WRAP initially focused on packaging and other materials that ended up in landfills, but in 2006 it sponsored a major research effort to determine the nature, scale, origin and causes of consumer food waste in the UK. These studies concluded that there was 'a genuine opportunity for the UK to take a lead in dealing with biowaste (i.e., food and organic garden waste) in Europe. It can learn from experience in other countries and manage biowaste more cost effectively and sustainably.'[11] WRAP's report, 'The Food We Waste' (2008), revealed that 6.7 million tonnes of food were thrown away each year in the UK, of which 4.1 million tonnes was avoidable. It concluded that UK consumers spent £10.2 billion on wasted food each year, which worked out to £420 of annual avoidable waste for the average household. Even householders who claimed that they generated no food waste produced on average 2.9 kilograms (6.4 lb) of it per week.[12] Since food prices were rapidly climbing at the same time, it was a timely message; the press and online sources played up the 'Shocking Food Waste Report', as it was headlined by one source.

As food prices continued to rise in 2008, WRAP hired Trimedia, a public relations firm, to launch a campaign encouraging consumers to reduce in-home food waste and keep food out of landfills. The campaign, called 'Love Food Hate Waste', was supported by leading chefs and food writers. It was kicked off at London's Borough Market, a major wholesale and retail food market that operated in accord with the campaign values and was accessible to journalists and film crews. By June 2008 the anti-food-waste advertising campaign had amassed more than 550 pieces of coverage in print and electronic media.

The success of Trimedia's public relations efforts gave the British prime minister Gordon Brown the opportunity to showcase food-waste reduction efforts at the G8 meeting of the world's major industrialized countries in July 2008. At the meeting Brown announced a forthcoming campaign to stamp out waste in the UK, declaring war on food waste as part of a global effort to curb spiralling food prices.

The prime minister's call for a war on food waste set the stage for several significant events beginning in 2009. The first was Defra Minister Hilary Benn's announcement of the construction of new biogas facilities in the UK that would produce fuel from organic waste via anaerobic digestion. Biogas, a renewable fuel, was an obvious solution when gas prices were high. When gas prices declined, the industry remained profitable thanks to improved technology and collection systems. Today, biogas facilities operate throughout the world – and many new facilities are under construction.

Benn also argued for an end to confusing expiration dates on packaged foods. The only useful label, Benn declared, was the 'use before' date, which was legally necessary for safety reasons. 'When we buy food it should be easy to know how long we should keep it for and how we should store it. Too many of us are putting things in the bin simply because we're not sure, we're confused by the label, or we're just playing safe.'[13] For the last decade, progress has been made among food manufacturers on this issue.

The second major event was the publication of *Waste: Uncovering the Global Food Scandal* in June 2009. Written by Tristram Stuart, a writer, dumpster diver, vegan and anti-food-waste activist, it contained jaw-dropping facts about food waste that came as a genuine shock to most readers. To help reduce and recycle food waste, Stuart founded an environmental non-profit organization called Feedback that, along with a coalition of other groups, staged 'Feeding the 5000' in London's Trafalgar Square on 16 December 2009.

Using only food recovered from supermarkets, bakeries and other sources, volunteers fed thousands of Londoners. The 'Feeding the 5000' feast garnered extensive media coverage, helping to focus the public's attention on the reduction of food waste. Stuart then starred in Olivier Lemaire's *Global Waste: The Scandal of Food Waste*, a documentary in which Stuart travelled from Europe to Ecuador, India, the u.s. and Japan targeting the food-waste culprits – food producers, industrialists, distributors and consumers – and also highlighting innovations and solutions for decreasing waste.

Food-waste reduction programmes were launched in many countries. Guillaume Garot, France's minister of agriculture, signed the National Pact (2013) to eliminate half of the nation's food waste by 2025. Arash Derambarsh, a city councillor of Courbevoie, France, started a 'field experiment' that acquired unsold supermarket food destined for the bin and distributed it to those in need. The experiment was so successful that Derambarsh launched a petition to demand a law be passed requiring supermarkets to donate edible food to hunger programmes. In just four months the petition attracted more than 200,000 signatures, along with French celebrity endorsements. Within a year, the French parliament passed a law banning supermarkets from throwing away edible excess food.

Ilse Aigner, the German minister for food, agriculture and consumer protection, funded an anti-food-waste campaign in 2010 with the slogan, 'Better Appreciation of the Value of Food!' This effort gained momentum when the University of Stuttgart reported that Germans wasted about 11 million tonnes of food annually, which worked out to 82 kilograms

(180 lb) per person per year, 60 per cent of it coming from private households. Peter Feller, the director of Germany's Federation of Food and Drink Industries, concluded that the main reason Germans discarded so much food was that food was 'too cheap'.[14] The German film-maker Valentin Thurn released the documentary *Taste the Waste*, followed by a book, *Die Essensvernichter* (The Food Destroyers). Thurn's work reports that European households throw away €100 billion worth of food every year, and that the amount of food wasted in Europe is 'enough to feed all the hungry people in the world two times over'. The film and book also highlight the fact that food rotting in garbage dumps has a disastrous impact on the world's climate.

Yet another major contributor to the war on food waste was the publication of Jonathan Bloom's *American Wasteland: How America Throws Away Nearly Half of Its Food (And What We Can Do About It)*, in 2010. Bloom, an American journalist, became interested in food waste while volunteering in a local food bank in Washington, DC. He created the 'Wasted Food' website, a blog and a Twitter feed, and began a speaking tour around the U.S. His book and continued activities alerted many Americans to the importance of reducing food waste.

The U.S. Environmental Protection Agency jumped on board the rapidly expanding anti-waste movement and proposed the Food Recovery Challenge in 2011. This initiative supported universities, businesses and other community organizations in making their food-management systems more sustainable. The Natural Resources Defense Council (NRDC) began publishing reports on food-waste-related topics, including Dana Gunders's 'Wasted: How America Is Losing Up to 40 Percent of Its Food from Farm to Fork to Landfill' (2012) and 'The Dating Game' (2013). Food Tank, a non-profit organization co-founded by Danielle Nierenberg and Ellen Gustafson, was started in 2013. The NRDC and Food Tank have continued to lead the promotion of anti-food-waste efforts ever since.

Petrol prices and food prices declined rapidly during the Great Recession, but by then anti-food-waste projects and programmes had been initiated by governments, non-profit organizations, for-profit businesses, foundations and concerned individuals around the world giving visibility to the issues and potential solutions. Start-ups, apps and platforms have been created to tackle food-waste reduction, recycling and reusing. Reports have concluded that food waste is a problem throughout food systems from food transporters and manufacturers to retailers and consumers. It begins on farms.

2
FARMED WASTE

From the time seeds sprout, plants are subjected to temperature fluctuations, lack of nutrients, too little or too much precipitation and damage caused by birds, rodents, diseases and insects. Harvesting is time-sensitive and often labour-intensive; a shortage of available trained labour at the right time can result in major crop losses. Post-harvest losses can be caused by malfunctioning farm equipment, handling and packing inefficiencies, problems related to storage facilities, lapses in refrigeration, poor processing techniques, improper fumigation, market or price fluctuations or institutional and legal obstacles.

During the twentieth century, food production was industrialized. Gas-powered farm equipment reduced the need for labour. The invention of chemical fertilizers, pesticides and the development of new crop varieties greatly increased productivity. Motorways, trains and container ships made it easier – and cheaper – to transport food from one part of the world to another. Farmers improved efficiency and enhanced production to meet global demand.

As farm production increased, however, so did food waste. The major cause was economics. Farming is a risky business. Farmers need to plan months or even years in advance.

They plant more than they anticipate selling, just to ensure a margin of safety, and harvest their crops when they can make the greatest profit. When the cost of harvesting crops exceeds the selling price, it makes no economic sense to continue harvesting.

The amount of food that is lost or wasted on farms and in transportation systems varies around the world. There are major differences between developing countries and industrialized countries. In developing regions, food loss on farms – and the loss in storing and transporting food to consumers – is massive. The main reason is the food loss caused by a lack of infrastructure, such as roads and storage facilities, and unreliable and erratic electricity (so cold storage facilities are limited). Governmental programmes and international aid groups have focused on improving transportation systems to move food supplies faster, and on faster food processing so less food is wasted.

In well-to-do countries, some food loss occurs at the production, storage and transportation stages, but most food is wasted due to planning failures or the overproduction of surplus food, particularly produce.

Gleaning Waste Away

An alternative to ploughing-under unharvested food is gleaning – the act of collecting leftover or unwanted crops, traditionally grains, after the main harvest is completed. Gleaning is an ancient custom that has been a part of agrarian societies for thousands of years, and it has been enshrined in religious traditions. Where permitted, gleaning of grains was a vital source of sustenance for large numbers of the working poor and the homeless, allowing them to put aside a little food in the autumn to get them through the winter.

During the late twentieth century gleaning re-emerged as a way to feed the needy. Newly organized programmes focused not on grains but on fresh fruit and vegetables. Today, gleaning programmes harvest tonnes of excess produce, simultaneously reducing waste and alleviating food insecurity. These programmes make fresh and nutritious fruits and vegetables available to the poor and undernourished. They are typically operated by volunteers, who may themselves be in need of food. These programmes 'empower individuals to participate in the process of securing food for themselves in a dignified and sustainable manner'.[1]

Organized gleaning operations in America gained visibility in 1979, when Second Harvest (later renamed Feeding America) was created in Arizona to help support food-assistance programmes. Its programme identified local farmers willing to permit gleaning, then organized volunteers to harvest crops after the farmers had completed their commercial harvests. Farmers received tax deductions for their donations. When the u.s. Congress examined gleaning in 1987, it concluded that it was a cost-effective supplemental tool to help feed the hungry, but that it could not replace hunger-relief programmes.

When food prices skyrocketed in the early twenty-first century, gleaning was promoted as part of the solution to food shortages, and hundreds of programmes were started or expanded around the world. In Canada dozens of gleaning programmes emerged, such as the LifeCycles Project, which coordinates a fruit-tree gleaning operation that gives one-quarter of the crop to the owners and the other three-quarters to the gleaners, who in turn give a portion to food banks. The Gleaning Network EU has established programmes in several European countries, including Belgium, Greece, France and Spain. In Australia, Continental, a Unilever food brand, partnered with RipeNear.Me to harvest and sell fresh fruit that was going unpicked on garden trees. The Gleaning Network UK, a programme of Feedback Global, was created in 2012 to coordinate volunteers, farmers and food-redistribution charities. Gleaning Hubs were established in London and Kent and other counties in England. Within four years these hubs rescued more than 3 million portions of fruit and vegetables.

Some projects convert surplus gleaned food into saleable products. Gleanings for the Hungry, for instance, manufactures millions of servings of dried soup mix using gleaned ingredients. The mix is distributed to food banks throughout the U.S. and is sent to other countries. Another organization, Gleaning the Harvest on Long Island, processes excess produce into 'added-value products' such as sauces, salsas, jams or jellies, which are distributed to food pantries.

Gleaning operations do not always run smoothly from the standpoint of hunger-relief programmes: there is uncertainty about when growers will open their land to gleaners and volunteer harvesters may not be available when needed. There is also the expense of driving workers to and from farms and feeding them if the work lasts more than an hour.

The gleaned products then have to be transported to food banks, and from there to local food pantries and soup kitchens. Despite their problems, there are thousands of gleaning programmes throughout the world today.

Produce Standards and Regulations

In Europe, legal standards for produce were established by the United Nations Economic Committee for Europe (UNECE). At the urging of food retailers, in 1980 the UNECE tasked the Working Party on Standardization of Perishable Produce with developing standards for fresh fruit and vegetables. The purpose was to promote trade in produce among European nations by creating voluntary quality standards. These included descriptions of acceptable shape, size and colour for 26 categories of fruit and vegetables, as well as standards related to health and safety. For example, Class 1 green asparagus had to be green for at least 80 per cent of its length, and cucumbers could not bend more than 10 millimetres for each 10 centimetres of their length. In 1988 the European Commission (EC) adopted the UNECE standards, which then became mandatory throughout the European Union. Produce that did not meet the lowest standards was typically converted into processed foods fed to livestock, or it was not harvested at all, and was instead ploughed under at the end of the season.

These regulations generated strong reactions: widespread support and widespread derision. Food retailers, farmers and farm organizations favoured the regulations, fearing that not setting standards would devalue their produce, thereby cutting their profits. Critics considered the standards absurd – yet another symbol of regulatory overkill by the EU. Retailers supported the EU regulations and developed similar in-house standards: they believed that customers would not buy misshapen, bruised, undersized or overripe fruit or vegetables, and so they refused to buy such produce from farmers. An estimated 20 to 40 per cent of all edible fresh produce was discarded or composted in the UK because it did not meet commercial standards, and it was calculated that these regulations added as much as 40 per cent to the price of some vegetables.[2]

When food prices rose dramatically during the early years of the twenty-first century, protests were heard from retailers and farmers. The growing barrage of negative press, as well as the rise in food prices, brought the EC's Management Committee for the Common Organisation of Agricultural Markets to reconsider these standards. It was thought that removal of the standards would lower the price of produce, and also decrease waste of fruit and vegetables – a topic that had surfaced in many EU countries. The Management Committee repealed all produce standards except those related to health and safety. The EC approved these changes in July 2009. Members of the EU were then able to buy and sell what had been previously defined as 'substandard' produce.

Despite the repeal, sales of irregular or misshapen fruit and vegetables have not increased appreciably. Some countries had their own national regulations that remained in effect. Large food retailers continued to adhere to their own standards, and customers were still put off by produce that was misshapen, discoloured, bruised or blemished.

Good, Bad and Ugly . . . Produce

Some crops, such as grains, can be stored until prices increase to a profitable level, but fruit and vegetables are a particular problem. When ripe, produce needs to be picked, processed and sold within short time spans. A study commissioned by the Natural Resources Defense Council found that up to 30 per cent of vegetable fields in the u.s. were not even harvested. Even in fields that *were* harvested, 1 to 4 per cent of the crop remained in the ground.[3] A survey conducted by Feedback, the organization founded in the United Kingdom by the anti-food-waste advocate Tristram Stuart, concluded that 10 to 16 per cent of the fruit and vegetables on uk farms were wasted.[4] Another report estimated that up to 40 per cent of all fruit and vegetables grown in the uk were rejected before reaching markets.[5] In total, about 50 per cent of produce grown in the u.s. was wasted.[6]

The major reason why fruit and vegetables are not harvested is that they do not meet buyers' specifications for size, shape, colour, ripeness, appearance and/or lack of blemishes. Agricultural workers are instructed not to pick them, and the unsaleable fruit and vegetables are ploughed under or converted into compost or animal feed. Producers and supermarket chains maintain these specifications because customers will not buy imperfect specimens even though they have the same nutritional value as flawless produce.

Imperfect produce from large farms can be sold to canning and freezing manufacturers or food service operators, where it is cut up and appearance doesn't matter. But that assumes that manufacturers are nearby and transportation costs are low. It also assumes that the varieties of produce grown are the ones manufacturers want. For farms with animals, excess and cosmetically challenged produce could be fed to the animals, provided the farmer had animals that ate produce. However, today many farmers do not raise animals and for them, surplus or late-maturing produce is typically ploughed under or turned into compost.

Wonky produce has been featured on television programmes. The British celebrity chefs Jimmy Doherty and Jamie Oliver hosted a Channel 4 programme on the 'ugly food' movement to make misshapen or bruised fruits and vegetables more acceptable to shoppers. As one farmer stated on the programme, 'Anything that doesn't make the grade gets chucked . . . Where "A" grade carrots sell for £800 a tonne, they practically give the ugly ones away for animal feed for just £10.'[7]

Hugh Fearnley-Whittingstall, the celebrity chef, television star and food writer, commenced his war on food waste in a three-part television series in 2015. The first episode, 'Why We Should Embrace Wonky Food', highlighted the waste caused by exacting supermarket standards. Fearnley-Whittingstall accompanied the series with a petition asking that viewers pledge to end food waste. This garnered 300,000 signatures, and major supermarkets took steps to increase sales of imperfect or 'wonky' produce. By November 2015, seven supermarket chains in the UK featured ugly produce. During the six months between filming the second and third episodes, the food redistribution charity FareShare received 60 per cent more food from retailers and manufacturers. Thanks to these contributions, FareShare announced, it was able to feed an extra 50,000 people every week. Asda featured six 'wonky' fruit and vegetable products, including crooked carrots, knobby pears and bumpy apples, that were bagged, labelled 'beautiful on the inside' and sold at significantly reduced prices. The UK's upscale supermarket chain Waitrose began selling weather-blemished and misshapen tomatoes, apples, pears, green beans, carrots, parsnips, potatoes and onions, branding them 'a little less than perfect'.

Similar programmes were launched in other countries. Imperfect Picks in Australia offers 'fruit and vegetables that might not look perfect from the outside, but are as perfect as ever on the inside'. Eroski, a Spanish supermarket chain, began selling 'less-than-perfect' produce under the label 'Tan Feas Como Buenas' (As Ugly As They Are Good). Dutch-based Delhaize offered 'Ugly Vegetable' boxes in many shops and announced that their produce managers would wait until older stock was sold before bringing out fresh items. The Fruta Feia (Ugly Fruit) Cooperative in Lisbon fought the 'dictatorship of aesthetics in fruits and vegetables' by selling produce rejected by grocery stores.

Intermarché, France's third-largest supermarket chain, began selling 'ugly' produce at a 30 per cent discount in 2014. It teamed up with Marcel, an advertising agency, to launch an ad campaign called 'Fruits et Légumes Moches' (Ugly Fruits and Vegetables). Billboards and advertisements on television, radio and social media platforms touted the benefits of imperfect produce. Ads featured the 'Ugly Carrot', 'Hideous Orange' and 'Failed Lemon'. 'Farm seconds' became popular overnight. Shortly afterward Intermarché offered a special sale of packaged baked goods with superficial imperfections. These items sold out quickly and traffic at Intermarché branches increased by an impressive 24 per cent. Other French supermarket chains now also sell discounted imperfect produce and other products, such as dated but edible baked goods.

In North America, anti-food-waste activist Jordan Figueiredo teamed up with nutritionist Stefanie Sacks to launch the 'Ugly Fruit and Veg Campaign' to convince supermarket chains to sell imperfect produce. Many have done so. Hy-Vee partnered with Robinson Fresh to create a line of 'Misfit' produce. Giant Eagle, a Pittsburgh-based food retailer, sells 'ugly' oranges, apples and potatoes. Canada's large supermarket chains – Safeway, IGA and Loblaws – have had success selling blemished or misshapen produce. Walmart, the world's largest food distributor, announced to great fanfare a pilot programme offering not-so-uniform potatoes they dubbed 'Spuglies'. Despite widespread praise, however, some chains have stopped ugly produce offers. Walmart discontinued selling bagged damaged apples labelled 'I'm Perfect', and Giant Eagle discontinued selling 'Produce with Personality'.

Waste caused by retailers' specifications also created opportunities for food delivery services to sell 'ugly' produce at greatly reduced prices. These programmes collect and bag the produce that cannot be sold to supermarkets and deliver it to members or subscribers. Chegworth Valley, a family-run fruit farm and juice maker in the UK, picks produce to order and makes next-day deliveries to restaurants. Wonky Vegetables, a start-up in Leicester, purchases vegetables discarded by processors and delivers them to retail customers.

They make a charitable donation for every delivery and also supply produce to food rescue organizations. London's Oddbox provides an outlet for 'imperfect' produce acquired from regional farmers. Members receive regular deliveries of healthful fruits and vegetables, and surplus produce is given to local food programmes to help feed those in need. Imperfect Produce, based in northern California, buys discounted fruits and vegetables that supermarket chains reject and sells them to customers at prices 25 to 50 per cent below what the supermarkets charge for perfect produce. Church Brothers Farms, in cooperation with the Compass Group North America, distributes Imperfectly Delicious Produce to hospitals, corporate cafés, universities, senior-living communities and restaurants. By 2016 the programme had reportedly saved £2 million worth of cosmetically challenged and underappreciated fruits and vegetables. The Culinary Misfits café in Berlin bought ugly produce from farmers and used it in its vegetarian menu items. These types of programmes have spread around the world and today are big business.

Not everyone agrees that upscale delivery services really reduce waste. Critics have complained that services selling ugly produce incentivize large-scale agribusinesses to overproduce to ensure that they can meet additional orders. They also note that food waste is a systemic problem – it can only be reduced when overproduction is curtailed. Others note that the ugly-produce movement represents a 'relatively small piece of the overall puzzle of action'.[8]

Upcycled Products

Recently, start-ups have appeared around the world to convert surplus or imperfect fruit and vegetables into recycled products. In Canada, LifeCycles processes the fruit into cider, jams, jellies, juice and other products and sells them to raise funds for the organization. The Fraser Valley Gleaners Society in British Columbia converts surplus produce into dried soup mixes and apple snacks that are distributed to food charities in forty countries around the world. Es Imperfect in Spain cooks up jams, soups and sauces using gleaned produce. Kromkommer (a play on the Dutch words for 'cucumber' and 'crooked') converts rejected vegetables into soups that are sold in 175 stores across the Netherlands. Gastromotiva, a non-profit hunger organization in Brazil, repurposes surplus food that was destined for the dump, turning it into granola, jam and dried banana snacks. San Francisco-based Full Harvest, for instance, acquires ugly produce from large farms and sells it to juicers and other manufacturers. Companies that sell, or make saleable products from, imperfect produce have helped farmers while also challenging supermarket cosmetic standards. Programmes that collect and distribute such produce may also make financial contributions to food banks.

ChicP in the UK makes sweet and savoury 'houmous' (humus) from rejected vegetables. Snact manufactures a line of snacks made from surplus fruit that would otherwise have been sent to landfill. Its products include fruit jerky made from apples sourced from farms in Kent and surplus

tropical fruit from wholesale markets. Snact pays for
the labourers to harvest the fruit, which gives farmers a
financial incentive to participate. Spare Fruit buys surplus
fruit from small farms and converts it into air-dried crisps.
Its profits go to transforming more surplus produce into
commercial products and to raising more awareness of food
waste. The British supermarket chain Tesco partnered with
organic dairy Yeo Valley and an organic fruit grower to convert imperfect apples into Apple and Custard Left-Yeovers
yoghurt. A portion of the profits go to food redistribution
charity FareShare. Flawsome! Drinks, in Cardiff, Wales,
takes rejected produce and converts it into 'marvellous' fruit
juice bottled in '100% recycled glass'. London's Dash Water
produces sparkling water infused with the juice of surplus
organic fruit and vegetables, including lemons from Sicily
and cucumbers from British farms. Fruit Magpie produces
traditional fruit 'cheeses' (firm, sliceable preserves) using
surplus produce from urban garden allotments. London-
based Rubies in the Rubble makes condiments, such as
relishes, jams and chutneys. They are trying 'to save the
planet one jar at a time', and promote their relishes with the
catchphrase, 'Some say it's a load of rubbish. We take that as
a condiment.'[9]

In America, wtrmln wtr in Colorado converts
'discarded watermelons' into beverages. It uses 99 per cent
of the entire melon and converts the rest into livestock feed.
In Washington, dc, FruitCycle transforms excess produce
from local farms into apple chips and kale chips, while jrink
Juicery and the Toki Underground have partnered to create
their own version of furikake, a rice seasoning, from ginger

pulp and kale stems. In Bethesda, Maryland, Full Plate Ventures produces tomato sauce, ratatouille, roasted bell peppers, frozen vegetables and apple sauce from surplus fruit and vegetables. Dieffenbach's Potato Chips in Womelsdorf, Pennsylvania, makes 'Uglies' from potatoes with minor imperfections; one of its slogans is 'Reducing Waste and Saving You Money'.

In Africa, a major waste problem is food spoilage, as many farmers do not have access to electricity. In Uganda, one proposed solution is the Sparky Dryer, a food dehydrator that runs on biofuel from garden waste. In Kenya, Azuri Health reduces post-harvest food losses on local farms by making and distributing dried fruit and vegetable products. Nigerian farmers dry surplus tomatoes and ship them to Spain, where chefs incorporate them into elegant chocolates.

These are just a few examples of the thousands of start-ups around the world that are upcycling what was once farmed waste.

Technovators to the Rescue?

Agricultural losses can be reduced by artificial intelligence technologies such as sensors, robots, drones, satellites and cameras that use algorithms for analysis. These provide farmers with detailed information on soil conditions, planting schedules, best varieties for the specific area and appropriate amounts of fertilizer, pesticide and water. This technology can communicate with other systems to reduce waste of agricultural inputs and increase food production. Sensors can also record temperature and humidity fluctuations in storage facilities and in transportation systems, such as shipping containers.

Other technologies help farmers and food companies to be more efficient in selling or donating surplus food. In the U.S., the apps CropMobster and Food Cowboy route surplus and unsaleable inventory to charities and food banks, and organic waste to composters. Donated food generates a tax deduction for the suppliers and food for those in need.

The Food for All Africa app in Ghana connects food retailers and smallholder farmers to help sell discounted and surplus food products. This limits farmers' financial losses and reduces waste. The excess food goes to low-income and vulnerable groups and institutions such as orphanages, hospitals and deprived communities.

New technology can also improve food storage and processing systems. The Rockefeller Foundation estimates that in Africa 20 per cent of cereals, 40 per cent of roots and tubers and 50 per cent of fruits and vegetables are lost in the post-harvest or processing stages. An estimated 45 per cent of that food spoils due to lack of cold storage. The company that manufactures ColdHubs, solar-powered walk-in cold rooms, states that the units are capable of extending the shelf life of produce and other perishable foods from two to 21 days and reducing post-harvest loss by 80 per cent.[10] Another solution is solar-powered devices, such as those manufactured by KinoSol, which produces solar-powered food dehydrators that need no electrical input. Its low-cost Orenda food dehydrator dehydrates fruits, vegetables, grains and insects that otherwise would be wasted.

Food processors are also using sensors to monitor performance indicators in real time. Once detected and flagged, problems can be managed so that waste is reduced. Amber Agriculture, an American for-profit AgTech company, developed sensors that can provide information on the condition of grain stored in silos by measuring temperature, humidity and other environmental conditions inside the structures. Data from the sensors is transmitted to the farmer via smartphones. Other apps help farmers determine the best time to sell and ship their crop.

New technology now on the drawing board could greatly reduce farmed food waste in the future. Michael Gove, the former UK secretary of the environment, believed that the world is entering an agricultural revolution due to accelerating technological advances that will increase productivity and reduce food waste, which he believes is 'an economic, environmental and moral scandal. We must end it.'[11]

New agricultural technology will likely improve agricultural productivity. The fight against food waste is a money-saving and money-generating opportunity for farmers. But it is not the panacea for ending food waste, as a large percentage of food waste is generated downstream in the food system by retail operations, service operators, consumers and manufacturers.

3
MANUFACTURED WASTE

For millennia people have collected, processed and stored foods when abundant for use in times of scarcity. From the moment food is harvested, picked, slaughtered or caught, it begins to deteriorate. From prehistoric times, humans have tackled the problem of how to preserve. Drying and salting were two of the earliest methods employed to keep food for later use. Immersion in wine, vinegar and oil were also techniques used for preserving food. Later developments included smoking or sugaring foodstuff, cooling food in cellars and freezing it with ice, where possible. Surplus food was fed to animals or was converted into compost, an extremely valuable commodity prior to the advent of chemical fertilizers in the twentieth century. Processing and storage systems failed occasionally, but edible food was not intentionally wasted.

Food production began industrializing in the late nineteenth century. As food manufacturers ramped up production volume, efficiency experts toured food plants to show management how to avoid waste, increase productivity and lower costs. Pork packers, for instance, proudly announced that their operations were the epitome of efficiency since they converted every by-product – even hair, hide, hooves and bones – into something useful. One pork packer boasted that his slaughterhouses used 'everything but the squeal'.

Improved Planning and Training

As industrialization decreased the cost of food during the twentieth century, manufacturers found it cheaper and more convenient to dispose of waste products rather than try to convert them into something saleable. Manufacturers tossed out food for many other reasons, including over-production, product deformities, machinery breakdowns, packaging damage, poor record-keeping and contamination. Researchers at Brunel University London and Ghent University investigated production processes at 47 food manufacturers in Belgium and found that human error accounted for about 11 per cent of all food waste.[1]

Food safety and contamination issues are also major causes of waste. Food can be contaminated with pathogens through failures in production processes. Chemical contamination with methylmercury, arsenic, melamine, urea and other substances has also occurred. If contaminated products get to the market-place, they can cause illness or even death and result in lawsuits and criminal prosecutions. As it is difficult to determine which batches of food have been affected, the manufacturer must recall all potentially tainted products, which can mean that thousands of items and millions of pounds' worth of good food products also have to be destroyed.

Safety issues caused product recalls in recent decades. In 2005 the British Food Standards Agency recalled 350 different food products that contained a red dye, known as Sudan 1, which was reportedly carcinogenic. The Hallmark/ Westland Meat Packing Company in California voluntarily recalled close to 65 million kilograms (143 million lb) of beef after a video surfaced showing unhealthy cattle being slaughtered without proper inspection, in violation of federal regulations. Recalls of 'potentially lethal' meat and poultry in the u.s. nearly doubled between 2013 and 2018. They varied from 80,000 kilograms (174,000 lb) of chicken wraps for possible listeria contamination to almost 5.5 million kilograms (12 million lb) of salmonella-tainted raw beef that sickened more than two hundred people.[2] A major reason for massive food recalls is the inability of producers, shippers, retailers and consumers to know precisely which food items are contaminated – so vast amounts of perfectly safe products are recalled and destroyed out of an abundance of caution.

During the past couple of decades, manufacturers have initiated internal programmes that reduce waste. Improved planning is one obvious solution. In the UK, a team examining the operation of Greencore's sandwich-manufacturing facility at Manton Wood, Nottinghamshire, found that the facility wasted tomato trimmings, leftover ham cuts and sausage ends, but the largest waste stream was bread (the ends of the bread were not used). The team recommended changes, which the company incorporated: the bread was repurposed as animal feed; tomato trimmings were used in recipes calling for diced tomatoes; sausage ends were used in stuffing; and ham waste was sent back to the supplier to be reused. Greencore also invested in new equipment that could prevent trimming waste. By making these changes the company cut an estimated 950 tonnes of annual waste.

In Ontario, Canada, Beau's Brewing Company launched a project in cooperation with the Commission for Environmental Cooperation and Enviro-Stewards to reduce loss. The prevention programme that emerged made it possible for Beau's to reduce waste, increase production by 7.4 per cent, and save C$722,000 per year.[3]

Greencore's and Beau's food waste reduction programmes are just two of the thousands underway by manufacturers throughout the world. Packers, manufacturers and transporters have substantially reduced waste in their operations – and generate substantial profits while doing so. One study, 'The Business Case for Reducing Food Loss and Waste' (2017), examined 1,200 businesses across the food supply chain, half of which carried out food-waste reduction programmes. For every $1 spent on reducing food waste, companies generated a profit of $14.[4]

Start-up Solutions

Yet another solution to decrease manufactured waste is distributing unused products to companies that can repurpose them. During the past decade thousands of start-ups have begun making consumer products using waste from food-processing facilities. Coffee waste is particularly adaptable to recycling. Brooklyn-based Nomad Trading Company bottles a line of beverages, called Cascara, that are brewed from coffee cherries (the fruit of the coffee tree, of which the coffee bean is the seed). Seattle-based CoffeeFlour sources coffee berries from small organic farms in Costa Rica, Nicaragua, Guatemala, Mexico, Vietnam and other countries; the dried fruit is ground into flour that can be used in baking and cooking. In Italy, RecoFunghi uses coffee grounds as a medium for growing mushrooms. GroCycle, in Devon, England, grows oyster mushrooms in coffee grounds. Wize Monkey in Vancouver, Canada, uses leaves from coffee trees to make 'coffee tea', which is sold in 35 countries.

Pulp from juice retailers is a widely recycled product. Pressed Juicery in San Diego makes veggie burgers from vegetable pulp for Mendocino Farms, an organic vegan restaurant chain near Los Angeles. Pulp Pantry turns pulp collected from juiceries into products such as pies, granola, crackers and baking mixes. Green Spot Technologies in Auckland, New Zealand, converts the pulpy waste of fruit and vegetables into apple, beetroot, orange and carrot flour. AquaBotanical in Australia 'harvests' and filters water produced when fruit and vegetables are juiced for concentrate, then bottles and sells it as a luxury bottled water.

Sir Kensington's, a Unilever subsidiary in the u.s., produces Fabanaise, a vegan mayonnaise made in part with aquafaba (the liquid in which dried chickpeas have been soaked), formerly discarded by hummus makers. Philabundance, a food recovery organization in Philadelphia, partners with TBJ Gourmet to produce a line of products called Abundantly Good. In San Francisco, the Forager Project bottles pressed vegetable juices; it makes snack chips with the solids left from juicing. ReGrained collects used grain from San Francisco-area brewers and transforms it into variously flavoured granola bars with names like 'IPA' and

'Chocolate Coffee Stout'. In California, Planetarians upcycles defatted seed cake by-products from cooking oil production into cooking ingredients and food products, such as Protein Chips. Renewal Mill manufactures a protein-rich soy flour from dried okara (soybean pulp that is a by-product of tofu and soy milk manufacture). The company's motto is 'Reducing food waste through creativity'.

Salt & Straw, a U.S. artisanal ice cream maker, uses food waste to create its 'Rescued Food Series'. Its Portland, Oregon, shop served up 'Urban Gleaners' Toasted Baguette PB&J',[5] made in part with leftover bread from local bakeries. Its Los Angeles outlet incorporated into its ice cream oranges, lemons, grapefruits and limes that gleaners have collected from garden fruit trees. Its San Francisco outlet came up with Roxie Road ice cream, made with leftover popcorn collected from the popping machines at the Roxie Theater.

Bananas are wasted more than any other type of produce. Spotted and surplus bananas and their peels can be used for animal fodder and compost, but vast quantities are binned. About 20 per cent of the bananas grown in Latin America have aesthetic shortcomings and cannot be exported. Barnana, a for-profit company based in Santa Monica, California, upcycles imperfect bananas into snack foods. Launched in 2012, within five years it was a multimillion-dollar company. In Queensland, Australia, Natural Evolution Foods transforms unsaleable bananas into gluten-free banana flour, a dietary fibre supplement and an anti-bacterial and anti-inflammatory ointment. Others have served fried banana peels at restaurants and still others have converted banana peels into cocktails, brownies, ethanol and many other products.

Tarac Technologies in South Australia is experimenting with grape marc – the seeds and skins left over from wine production – as food for farmed abalone. It also uses marc in other value-added products such as stock feed, compost and grape seed extract. In Israel, Wine Water Ltd combines spring water with the leftovers from the Golan Heights Winery to make O.Vine, a non-alcoholic beverage that touts 'an intoxicating aroma and refreshing taste'. The Dutch company De Verspillingsfabriek – 'The Waste Factory' – uses 'deformed' fruits and vegetables, and rescued meat scraps from wholesalers, farmers, auctions and food processors, to make heat-and-eat soups. De Verspillingsfabriek and the supermarket chain Plus have embarked on a joint project to convert overripe produce into products called OverLekker (Beyond Delicious).

Feeding discarded food to animals is hardly a new idea, but technology has taken it far beyond slopping pigs with kitchen scraps. Shandong Qiaobin in Jinan, China, uses cockroaches to convert food waste into animal feed. Nutrinsic, a Denver-based company, partnered with MillerCoors to convert used grains and yeast into proteins used for fish food. Brewery waste is also used to feed black soldier fly larvae (*Hermetia illucens*), which eat double their weight every day. The larvae are then sold live or dried as feed for poultry, fish and turtles, and the remains of the food wastes are used for fertilizer. Grubbly Farms in Georgia and Mad Agriculture in Boulder, Colorado, raise black soldier fly larvae on leftover juice pulp and used brewers' grains to make chicken feed. Similarly, AgriProtein in Cape Town, South Africa, also feeds fly larvae on food waste to make fish pellets and pet foods. Insect larvae are also raised on waste for animal food in many other countries.

Alcoholic Solutions

Just as spent grains and other by-products of alcoholic beverage production are being upcycled, waste from other food industries has become the basis of beers, wines and spirits. In England and Wales, Toast Ale makes beer from discarded bread. 'It's the best thing since sliced bread,' quipped Anthony Bourdain in the film *Wasted! The Story of Food Waste* (2017). The brewery waste is fed to pigs. On the Bolney Wine Estate in Sussex, England, Foxhole Spirits 'second-presses' surplus grape juice from the winery, adds grapes that are damaged, wrinkled or fail to meet supermarket specifications, and ferments it into 'English wine' and Hyke Gin. Seven Bro7hers in Manchester made craft beers – 'Throw Away IPA', 'Cast Off Pale Ale' and 'Sling It Out Stout' – from Kellogg's Cornflakes, Rice Krispies and Coco Pops that had been rejected because they were too big, too small, overcooked or otherwise imperfect.

In the U.S., companies such as Ventura Spirits and Misadventure Vodka distil spirits from surplus food and food waste. Imperfect strawberries form the basis of Ventura's brandy and vodka. The company claims that during the first three years of production it diverted 500,000 strawberries from the waste stream. Misadventure claims that drinking its vodka promotes 'hedonistic sustainability' so you can 'enjoy yourself while doing good'. In Oregon, Wheyward Spirit partners with dairies to repurpose leftover whey into a vodka-like spirit. Been a Slice in Toronto, Canada, brews surplus bread into a small-batch beer that is sold to restaurants and bars. The proceeds from the sales are donated to Second Harvest, a Canadian food rescue organization. Singapore researchers converted tofu whey, a liquid waste, into an alcoholic product they named Sachi, a Japanese word meaning 'the blossoming of flowers and wisdom'.

Perhaps the most unusual waste-based alcoholic product was Pisner beer, produced in 2017 in a limited release of just 60,000 bottles by the Danish microbrewery Nørrebro Bryghus. Two years earlier, the brewery had fertilized fields of barley with urine collected from urinals at Northern Europe's largest music festival. The barley was then malted and used to brew Pisner beer.

Non-edible Solutions

And not everything made from food manufacturers' waste is destined for the table. H. J. Heinz, the world's largest ketchup maker, has worked with the Ford Motor Company to convert leftover tomato fibre into bioplastics for use in storage compartments of cars. In addition, Ford takes recycled coffee chaff from McDonald's and converts it into the plastic headlamp housings on cars. In the Philippines, Piñatex makes a strong, flexible, leather-like material from pineapple leaf fibres. It is used to manufacture a variety of products, from shoes to furniture. Madagascar's Flore Aroma converts biodegradable green waste – flower cuttings, hedge

trimmings and commercial food waste – into mosquito and
fly repellent, air fresheners, shampoo, shower gel, soaps and
deodorants. Orange Fibre in Italy transforms citrus peels into
a soft, silky fabric used by Salvatore Ferragamo, an Italian
luxury goods company.

Coffee grounds can also be turned into furniture frames,
coffee cups, fabric, clothes, furniture, jewellery, lamps, toys
and printing ink. Other companies convert cow stomachs
into shoes and fish skin into eyeglass frames, slippers and
bags. Edible containers are fashioned from tomato skins
and tea leaves; sponges from tequila distillery waste; textiles
from milk casein; leather from grape marc; brushes from
eggshells or fruit peels; packaging materials from eggs and
coconut fibres. London-based Aeropowder converts feathers
from the poultry industry into packaging insulators, while
Circular Systems in Los Angeles converts waste such as sugar
cane fibre, pineapple leaves, banana trunks and hemp stalks,
into cheap textile fibres for the fashion industry. At the City
University of Hong Kong, coffee grounds and other waste
products are used to fertilize organically grown mushrooms
that are then served at the Sheraton Hotel. Ohio State
University researchers have synthesized rubber suitable
for vehicle tyres from eggshells and tomato peels.

In Europe, researchers have found a way to convert the
wastewater from juice processing to make PHBOTTLE, a biodegradable bioplastic. Spanish researchers at the University
of Granada have used absorbent materials made from orange
and grapefruit peels to purify water containing heavy metals
and organic compounds that are considered pollutants.
Optiat (an acronym for 'One Person's Trash Is Another's

Treasure') in the UK turns coffee grounds into skincare products. The London firm bio-bean converts waste coffee grounds into biomass pellets and logs to fuel fireplaces, furnaces and cookstoves, and has experimented with making biodiesel from coffee grounds. Scientists at the Royal Belgian Institute of Natural Sciences have used shells from farmed molluscs to help restore reefs and reduce acidity in soil.

In Edinburgh, Scotland, Celtic Renewables combines the two main by-products of whisky-making – pot ale (the liquid residue from a still) and draff (protein-rich barley malt residue) – to produce renewable fuels, including biobutanol, which can be blended with petrol and used to power vehicles. A New Zealand brewery, DB Export, uses leftover yeast to make a clean-burning biofuel called 'Brewtroleum' that is sold in gas stations. Brewtroleum was promoted with the line, 'Drink Beer, Save the World!'

Other non-edible products made from the waste produced by food manufacturing include biodegradable and compostable lamps, bowls and jackets made from coconut shells and husks; paper made partially from citrus, kiwifruit, corn, beans, olives and nut waste; planters made from dried gourds and mushrooms; and tableware made from sugar-cane stalks.

Ending Label Waste

When manufacturers began selling own-brand canned, bottled, bagged and boxed goods, the packaging preserved the food and prevented spoilage for a reasonable period of time, but the products eventually began to deteriorate, and the consumer might not have known this until the package was opened. During the mid-twentieth century, food manufacturers began using dating systems that placed numerical codes or symbols on packages to identify the date and time of production. These were used by distributors and retailers to manage inventory, rotate stock and assist in product recalls. These codes also informed retailers of the need to sell or discard packaged foods before they passed their prime, thereby protecting businesses from potential complaints or litigation from customers made ill by spoiled food.

Different systems were employed around the world, and since many food products are exported, these diverse systems caused confusion among consumers. By the 1970s many countries, international organizations and multinational food manufacturers and retailers required product dating, particularly for foods with a short shelf life (such as milk) and products intended for export. Companies around the world began marking packaged foods with freshness indicators, such as 'use by', 'best before', 'enjoy by', 'sell by' and 'display until'. This was called 'open dating', meaning that it was not encoded and could be understood by anyone. Each company developed its own system, and eventually more than fifty different date-labelling systems emerged worldwide; in some countries, such as the u.s., food processors developed multiple systems to comply with varying state and local laws.

Because food quality can be affected by factors other than time, such as temperature, humidity and light, the dates were approximate. A u.s. Department of Agriculture survey in 1971 showed that 20 per cent of those surveyed had complaints about the freshness of packaged and canned foods and beverages; a Nielson opinion survey turned up 50 per cent with such complaints. By 1973 ten states had adopted legislation that required 'sell-by' or other dates on certain types of food, 'even though it was widely recognised that this would not assure the microbiological safety of food'.[6] Other surveys found that 89 per cent of consumers who responded favoured a simplified product-dating system.[7] No datelabelling system has been mandated nationwide in the United States, except for infant formula, although most states have established dating requirements and some impose fines on businesses that sell food on or after its expiration date.

Date labelling gave guidance about when packaged food might no longer be at its best, but retailers and customers alike sometimes interpreted the dates as law and discarded foods that had neared or passed their freshness dates. Food dating has increasingly become an issue over the past decade. A 2008 survey by the Waste and Resources Action Programme (WRAP) found that '53 per cent of British consumers did not eat fruit or vegetables that exceeded the "best before" date; 56 per cent did not eat bread or cake; and 21 per cent never even "take a risk" with food close to its date.'[8] A 2010 WRAP report revealed that about 450,000 tonnes of food was thrown away because it had passed a 'best before' date. Had the food been stored properly, it would have been perfectly safe to eat up to and after this date. The report also estimated that 380,000 tonnes of food was tossed out because it had passed a 'use-by' date – waste that could have been avoided had the food been cooked or frozen before that date. A study by Approved Food, an online retailer of short-dated and residual stock food and beverages in Scotland, showed that more than 50 per cent of the country's population threw away perfectly edible food that was approaching or past its 'best before' date, and that 62 per cent of this group did so because they feared becoming ill.

A Belgian study found that 30 per cent of those surveyed did not know the difference between 'use by' and 'best before' labels. Research conducted in the Netherlands revealed that 15 per cent of food waste was caused by misunderstanding food package labels. The European Commission found that fewer than half of those surveyed knew the meaning of 'best before' labels. Most consumers believed that food with an expired 'best before' date should not be eaten. A German study showed that changing labels on some grocery products (pasta and canned food) from 'best before' to 'long life' could slash the amount of discarded food by more than 30 per cent.

More than one-third of Americans routinely discarded food close to or past the date on the label, and 84 per cent did so at least occasionally, reported a study by the Harvard Food Law and Policy Clinic and the Natural Resources Defense Council in 2013. It found that 91 per cent of consumers threw out food based on the 'sell-by' date out of a mistaken concern for food safety. This costs households an estimated $275 to $455 per year. The study concluded that labelling systems were confusing and that they were a major factor in the loss of an estimated 72.5 billion kilograms (160 billion lb) of food in the U.S. every year. Emily Broad Leib, the lead author, argued for 'a standardized, common-sense date labelling system that actually provides useful information to consumers, rather than the unreliable, inconsistent and piecemeal system we have today.'[9] Leib's work on food expiration dates was subsequently converted into the documentary *Expired? Food Waste in America* (2016).

The Consumer Goods Forum – a coalition of more than four hundred companies in seventy countries – formed a voluntary initiative to standardize date labels. Specifically, they proposed that by 2020 members would limit themselves to just two labels: 'use by', an expiration date for product safety, and 'best if used by', a food quality label that would apply to non-perishable items like canned goods. While this is an important step, local and national laws need to be adjusted before this uniform system can achieve maximum success.

New food-labelling guidelines have been launched in many countries. A two-label system has been recommended in the UK: 'best before' labels would refer to best food quality and 'use-by' date labels would indicate that a product is safe to consume up to that date. Food can be sold after its 'best before' date has passed, providing the product's packaging is undamaged. The Norwegian discounter REMA 1000 added 'often good after' to 'best before' labels on its canned food, eggs, dairy and dry foods. The Danish-based non-profit Too Good to Go partnered with food manufacturers, including Unilever, Arla, Løgismose Meyers, Coop and Carlsberg, to replace 'best before' dates with 'often good after' on milk, beer, chocolate and other products. Too Good to Go also petitioned national food regulators to make similar labelling changes. In May 2019 the U.S. Food and Drug Administration recommended that the food-processing industries use the term 'best if used by' date label.

Labels may well become less important if current technology is incorporated into food packages. Smart label techniques have emerged that include visual indicators that provide information about the quality of the food, its storage history, and its state of freshness or deterioration. They can show the level of ripeness in fruit, for instance, and whether there have been gaps in the refrigeration of vegetables. This system is more accurate than pre-set 'best before' dates and gives confidence to retailers and customers that freshness or sell-by dates may not provide.

Smart labels combine new technologies: QR codes, sensors, microchips, radio-frequency identification (RFID) tags and optical character recognition (OCR) tags. Some smart labels change colour to indicate spoilage or contamination by bacteria. Sainsbury's, the UK supermarket chain, is field-testing a new label, 'smart Fresh', that changes colour from yellow to purple when food is beginning to spoil. Another technology that may eliminate the need for date labels is freshness detectors, such as paper-based electrical gas sensors (PEGS). These paper-based biodegradable sensors are carbon electrodes that are printed into cellulose paper and incorporated into the packaging, which changes colour as the food in the package deteriorates.

Yet another solution is the 'Bump Mark', a bio-reactive food expiration label. It was invented by Solveiga Pakštaité at Brunel University London in 2014. Searching for ways to help visually impaired people determine whether packaged food was safe to consume, Pakštaité came up with a tactile solution: she incorporated material into the label, a gelatin that deteriorates at the same rate as proteins in foods. A smooth surface on a package with the Bump Mark indicates that the food inside is fresh and wholesome; a bumpy surface warns that the food may not be safe to eat.

Reducing Storage and Transport Waste

Today, food systems are global. About 40 per cent of the food transported needs refrigeration and about 20 per cent of food loss is caused by equipment and communication breakdowns. A food product can change hands as many as 33 times before reaching consumers. Miscommunication at any stage can cause needless food waste. For instance, more than 37,000 tonnes of bananas were lost in Australia in the late 1990s due to the lack of communication between growers and packers.

Storage and transportation breakdowns cause losses, but new technology can reduce this waste. Maintaining temperature control in transit from the point of harvest, slaughter or processing to the point of sale maintains the condition, flavour and nutritional value of meat, fish, dairy and produce, and to this end temperature-controlled supply systems called 'cold chains' have been adopted around the world. Vegetables, for instance, are cooled immediately after harvest, then transported in a continuous chain of refrigerated and ventilated containers and vehicles to keep them fresh all the way to the market. Cold chains make it possible to transport perishable goods thousands of kilometres to enable out-of-season sales in distant markets. Use of cold chain technology can reduce food loss by as much as 76 per cent.[10]

Recent technological advances have dramatically improved cold-chain monitoring and control. Biosensors and trackers that use radio-frequency identification (RFID) can substantially reduce food waste during transportation and storage. Wireless sensors, such as those developed by VTT Technical Research Center, headquartered in Espoo, Finland, can detect ethanol in the headspace of food packaging, allowing live data on the food's quality and freshness to be transmitted via RFID tag technologies. These sensors monitor food quality, nutritional value and safety from the farm to the table throughout the distribution chain, reducing the amount of food wasted during transportation. A system called BT9 xsense, developed in Israel, monitors, analyses and disseminates relevant quality data and recommendations throughout the entire cold chain. A report by the World Economic Forum on traceability concluded that application of sensor-based technology in the food supply chain decreased food waste in the transportation system by 5 to 7 per cent.[11]

Other solutions to reduce food waste in the storage and transportation sectors are the use of artificial intelligence technology, machine learning and data science. San Francisco-based AgShift uses 'deep learning' to inspect nuts and seafood. Boston-based Spoiler Alert helps large food manufacturers and distributors better manage their inventory to optimize purchasing, accounting and reporting systems to capture tax benefits. Cheetah, a smartphone app developed by Ujuizi Laboratories (based in the Netherlands and Ghana), steers farmers, food transporters and traders to the fastest travel routes in order to avoid delays. It is used in much of Africa.

Blockchain technology, a decentralized record-keeping system, permits traceability and can greatly reduce waste in food systems. It tells users where food or food products came from, how they were grown, raised, caught or processed, the temperatures at which they were stored, where ordered products are in the supply chain, and so on. Once safety problems are identified, blockchain technology can locate the source and find all products that may have safety issues. This can keep perfectly safe food from being recalled due to lack of traceability.

Blockchain technology can prevent food loss due to miscommunication within the logistics supply chain. Currently, growers, shippers, packers and sellers base orders on estimates for demand based on incomplete information. Large supermarket chains, such as Walmart, Unilever and Carrefour, are experimenting with blockchain applications to help track food supply chains, improve food safety recalls and minimize waste. Using such systems has meant that large food retailers can reduce transport time – in some cases by 50 per cent – and thus lengthen the in-store shelf life of fresh fruit items. By 2019 more than 5 million products were being tracked using blockchain technology.

High-tech labels can also provide traceability of products from producer to consumer. Fishpeople Seafood, based in the American Pacific Northwest, has created labels with numbers that identify precisely where the fish was caught – and who caught it. All the customer has to do is type the package number into the company's website to get this information.

Smart sensors now travel with food from the farm to the supermarket. The Swiss Federal Laboratories for Materials

Science and Technology has developed sensors to monitor the state of fruit during travel. Centaur Analytics in Greece has developed wireless sensors designed to 'sniff' crop-storage conditions inside shipping containers, grain bins and storage bunkers. Zest Labs in California has developed similar technology to send an alert if warehoused produce is ripening faster than anticipated, so that it can be re-routed to a closer outlet and still retain a good shelf life. Zest Labs claims that this technology saves about 9 per cent of produce that would ordinarily go to waste. Smart sensors also record temperatures during transit and supply information about the freshness of incoming produce, helping managers calculate when and how to sell the produce and at what price, in order to maximize sales and minimize waste.

Hundreds of major food and beverage companies, including Campbell's, Unilever, Nestlé and Anheuser-Busch InBev, have committed to halving the remaining food waste within their operations by 2025. Other companies, such as Cranswick, one of the UK's largest food producers and suppliers, are committed to become 'waste-free' businesses by 2030.

4
SUPERMARKET WASTE

Grocery chains were born during the late nineteenth century. These multi-store operations had the advantage of purchasing goods in bulk and selling them more cheaply than small independent grocers could. Supermarkets – large, self-service grocery stores that sold tens of thousands of items, providing one-stop shopping – proliferated after the Second World War. Customers who had previously made the rounds of bakeries, butchers, greengrocers and other speciality stores could buy all their food in one place, and most supermarkets had spacious car parks, so suburbanites could ferry home a week's worth of food in one trip. During the last decades of the twentieth century, supermarket chains consolidated and a small number of megacorporations began to dominate national grocery sales. Companies expanded operations outside of their country of origin, creating multi-national supermarket chains that dominate grocery sales in multiple countries.

Retailers anticipate demand and meet consumer expectations. Waste occurs when managers misjudge the demand for certain products and end up with overstock. Workers recheck product labels on cans and packages and those items nearing 'best before' dates are discarded.

Supermarket managers also ditch outdated promotional items, unpopular products, damaged packages and items returned by customers.

Waste is also generated by baking operations and ready-to-eat food sold in supermarkets. Because the aroma of baking attracts customers, supermarkets with bakeries keep turning out fresh bread well into the evening, even if the product has to be dumped when the store closes. Ready-to-eat food from in-store operations, such as rotis-serie chickens, sandwiches, salad bars and the like, poses similar problems.

Produce departments are major waste centres. They typically feature bountiful displays of perfectly shaped and coloured fruit and vegetables. Staff restock the produce sec-tion every day to make sure it looks fresh and appealing. Old, soft, undersized, bruised, blemished or discoloured items go into the bin. The cost of waste management, such as remov-ing, disposing of, recording and reordering replacements, amounts to only a fraction of the total cost of food. Those costs are calculated into the retail price of groceries.

Freegans, Dumpster Diving, Bin Raiding, Skipping

By the 1960s supermarkets and food-service operations were dumping astronomical quantities of edible food into the garbage. Fruit, vegetables, baked goods, meat and dairy past their prime, as well as packaged goods that were damaged or close to their sell-by dates, were tossed into dumpsters (big metal trash receptacles, also known as 'bins' or 'skips') along with packing crates, boxes, bottles and other such items.

Dumpsters were picked up and emptied into garbage trucks, which then carried the refuse to landfill sites.

Piled high with edible food, the dumpsters left outside supermarkets at night did not go unnoticed. The homeless, the poor and the hungry foraged in the containers for anything edible. The Diggers, an anarchist group based in San Francisco's Haight-Ashbury district, started organizing food-scavenging expeditions to grocery stores, produce markets and other food-service operations in 1967. They also received donations from farmers. The Diggers cooked up their gleaned ingredients in a huge pot, and the resulting 'Digger Stew' and fresh fruit were offered to all comers in Golden Gate Park every day at four o'clock. Surplus food was also given away. Digger Stew faded when the 'Summer of Love' ended in 1968, but the concept of picking through bins for edible food has lived on.

Keith McHenry, an anti-nuclear activist, helped found 'Food Not Bombs' in 1980. One of the group's activities was to recover food from dumpsters behind supermarkets and elsewhere. McHenry is credited with coining the term 'freegan', a combination of 'free' and 'vegan'. Freegans typically live outside the conventional market economy and believe that society is rife with materialism, consumerism and moral apathy. They seek to undermine capitalist enterprises by living off the waste that businesses produce. As one freegan slogan goes, 'We'll eat your scrap, but we won't buy your crap.'[1]

Using scavenged groceries, freegans provided vegan meals to anyone who showed up at protest rallies and other public events, offering 'solidarity, not charity'. The concepts and methods behind freeganism quickly spread throughout the world. A group of activists in New York City put up a website and formed an organization called 'freegan.info'. They hosted 'trash tours' of the city and sought visibility in print and electronic media. Freegans, they averred, were no longer radical anti-capitalists but people who believe in ethical consumption and reject the waste of food and other resources. As one observer noted, however, many were just people who preferred to get their food for free.

Freegans operate under a code: 'You don't take more than you can use and you leave the place clean. You never take all the food in case someone else looks after you do.'[2] Not all 'dumpster divers' adhered to that creed, and supermarket managers became concerned with liability issues related to the food tossed into their garbage bins.

Supermarkets took steps to prevent or discourage scavenging, hiring nightwatchmen to patrol outdoor areas and placing locks on the bins to prevent pilfering. Some businesses poured bleach or other caustic chemicals on discarded food to render it inedible. One British supermarket padlocked its bins and concealed them behind a metal gate complete with repelling spikes.

Dumpster diving generated press reports, and soon academics commenced investigating it. Jeff Ferrell, a tenured professor, quit his job and for eight months survived on discarded food found on the streets of Fort Worth, Texas. He published his experiences in *Empire of Scrounge: Inside the Urban Underground of Dumpster Diving, Trash Picking, and Street Scavenging* (2005). Four years later the Oklahoma University Press released *Going Green: True Tales from Gleaners, Scavengers, and Dumpster Divers*. Numerous articles about dumpster diving have appeared in academic journals, magazines, newspapers and online posts. Masters theses and dissertations have been written on the subject, and video clips of dumpster diving are frequently posted on YouTube and elsewhere online.

While most dumpster divers say they are doing so to feed themselves and others, some have claimed that they have generated tidy sums by selling what they have recovered. In the 1980s James Jugan, a New Jersey resident, began 'recycling' products, including food, from dumpsters and then selling them at 25 per cent off their list price. He claims to have earned $100,000 a year doing this. Others reported that they made $30,000 per year. These 'professional' dumpster divers claim that their for-profit businesses were declining because amateurs were siphoning off goodies due to all the publicity.

Countries differ in their laws regulating dumpster diving. It is legal in the u.s. except where prohibited by local laws. In Germany, on the other hand, food in dumpsters remains the property of the supermarket until waste collectors take it away. Anyone engaged in dumpster diving (*Containern* or *Mülltauchen*) at German supermarkets is stealing – and people have been charged and convicted under this law. Dumpster diving is also illegal in other countries, including Belgium and the uk.

Some business owners called on the police to arrest dumpster divers. A woman named Sasha Hall was taken to court by uk supermarket giant Tesco and charged with theft for taking food from one of the chain's waste bins in 2011. Hall faced a six-month prison sentence or a £5,000 fine. The case received widespread publicity, including a Facebook page urging a boycott of Tesco. The court released Hall on the condition that she refrain from engaging in such activity in the future. In 2014 three men were arrested behind an Iceland supermarket in north London when they were found removing food from dumpsters. They were charged with violating the 1824 Vagrancy Act but the Crown Prosecution Service dropped the charges, concluding that it was 'not in the public interest' to prosecute them.

Freegans have filmed their exploits acquiring food from supermarket bins and serving meals prepared with groceries 'liberated' from waste receptacles and posted these videos on YouTube. The ensuing attention caused public relations nightmares for supermarkets. Then professional film-makers jumped in. American film-maker Jeremy Seifert filmed divers who salvaged thousands of dollars' worth of edible food behind Los Angeles supermarkets. He confronted supermarket executives, urging them to donate more food to local food banks. Managers of food banks thanked Seifert as they reported big jumps in donations from local supermarkets. Seifert's documentary *Dive!* (2009) ends with a quotation from Noam Chomsky, the philosopher, social critic and political activist: 'Change doesn't trickle down from above, it grows from below.'

As a consequence of potential public relations concerns, supermarkets rarely involve the police anymore and there have been relatively few arrests and convictions for taking discarded food out of the garbage. Supermarkets have reduced the amount of edible food tossed into dumpsters by developing programmes to distribute it to food banks and other initiatives that help feed the needy.

Legal Issues

Beginning in the 1980s, food retailers began donating 'short dated' packaged goods to food banks, soup kitchens and local food pantries that distribute food directly to those in need. This raised the potential of lawsuits if those who ate the food became ill. During the 1990s laws were passed in many cities, states and provinces, protecting the donor from liability if adverse consequences resulted from donations given in good faith. The u.s. Congress passed the Model Good Samaritan Food Donation Act in 1990 and the Bill Emerson Good Samaritan Food Donation Act in 1996 to encourage donation of food and grocery products to non-profit organizations without the fear of liability. Italy became the first European country to pass a Good Samaritan Law (Law No. 155/2003) in July 2003. On 16 October 2017 the European Union adopted the Food Donation Guidelines, which encouraged food manufacturers and retailers to donate their surplus to food banks and charities.

Similar laws were passed elsewhere, limiting criminal and civil liability for those who made donations in good faith and encouraging food processors, restaurateurs and food-service companies to donate edible food that would otherwise go to waste. The laws also helped develop procedures for safe food handling and storage of donated food to food banks. Countries including Greece, France, Hungary, Finland and Turkey now offer tax deductions to companies that give food to food banks, Salvation Army programmes and other charities.

It is not in the financial self-interest of retailers to throw away edible food. Neither is it in their interest to be publicly criticized for discarding wholesome, nourishing food when people in their local communities are going hungry. When reports of supermarket waste surfaced in the 1990s, some grocery chains publicly supported anti-waste efforts. By 1998 UK food retailers such as Marks & Spencer were donating large quantities of excess food to feed the hungry. This turned out to be a public relations boon for those retailers.

Supermarket Waste Wars

In the face of revelations about how much usable food they were throwing away, UK supermarkets claimed in 2008 that they gave most of their surplus food to charity. The Sainsbury's supermarket chain, for instance, reported donations of 6,680 tons of food in the 2006/7 fiscal year. However, this represented only 10 per cent of what they discarded per annum. Another UK chain, Tesco, had reportedly dumped an estimated 125,000 tonnes of food.[3]

When the British prime minister Gordon Brown announced a war on food waste in 2008, Kath Dalmeny, Policy Director of Sustain (an alliance of one hundred national public-interest organizations in the UK), called on the prime minister to play a leading role in reducing supermarket waste. Steve Webb, environment spokesman for the Liberal Democrats, blamed food waste partly on the government's

cosy relationship with the big chains [that] has stalled effective action . . . Supermarkets make it harder for householders to avoid food waste, while throwing away large quantities of edible food through poor stock management. They refuse to stock small portions, which are essential for the growing number of one-person households, and offer too many buy-one-get-one-free deals on perishable goods.[4]

A Sainsbury executive reacted to Webb's claims this way: 'We'll consider lessons from politicians on how to run our supply chains, in the same way that politicians would take lessons from us on how to deal with their constituents.'[5]

Another notable figure in the fight against supermarket food waste was Tristram Stuart, who, while a student at Trinity Hall, Cambridge, took to raiding the rubbish bins at Sainsbury's. He brought back discarded cheese, yoghurt, fresh produce and other food. Stuart continued to 'liberate' edible supermarket discards throughout his college years, and after graduation he organized a media campaign targeting this egregious waste. He took radio and television crews to the backs of supermarkets and, with the reporters, examined what was being thrown out. Stuart's book *Waste: Uncovering the Global Food Scandal* carried an indictment of supermarket policies. He demonstrated that most food discarded by UK supermarkets went straight into landfill sites. Stuart wrote:

All this may ironically have contributed to the cornucopian abundance that has fostered a culture in which staggering levels of 'deliberate' food waste are now accepted or even institutionalised. Throwing away cosmetically 'imperfect' produce on farms, discarding edible fish at sea, over-ordering stock for supermarkets, and purchasing or cooking too much food in the home, are all examples of profligate negligence toward food.[6]

The staff of the Canadian Broadcasting Corporation (CBC) entered the supermarket anti-waste campaign when its 'News Marketplace' and 'Go Public' programmes launched an investigation of food waste behind Walmart stores in Ontario and other Canadian provinces. Making multiple visits to Walmart waste bins over a six-month period, researchers 'repeatedly found produce, baked goods, frozen foods, meat and dairy products'. Most food 'was still in its packaging, rather than separated for composting . . . bottles of water, frozen cherries that were still cold and tubs of margarine . . . In many cases, however, the food was well before its best-before date and appeared to be fresh.' The CBC investigators concluded that they had seen only a small portion of the discarded food, as many stores had trash compactors that made it impossible to determine how much food was actually thrown away. Daniel Schoeler, who had worked at almost a dozen Walmarts in the Vancouver area, told reporters, 'It's heartbreaking when you go home at the end of the day, to see that much food get thrown out.'[7]

After the CBC stories aired, beginning in October 2016, Walmart claimed that the food in their bins was unfit to eat and that some items had been returned by customers after purchase and thus could not be resold. Some Walmart store managers responded by locking their garbage bins. Current and former employees of Walmart, however, confirmed that large amounts of food were routinely discarded. Walmart executives finally acknowledged their mistakes and vowed to change the supermarket's food waste policies. A year later, Walmart announced that it had reduced food waste by 20 per cent since the CBC investigation.[8]

Supermarket Programmes and Donations

Supermarkets responded to the continued onslaught of negative publicity by increasing their donations to food banks and reducing the amount of food sent to landfill, and most have programmes that donate food to charities. In the U.S., Target, Sam's Club and Walmart, in partnership with the hunger charity Feeding America, began donating millions of kilograms of excess stock to food pantries. In Canada, Walmart and the Loblaws chain reported that they had diverted 'more than 14 million pounds of safe quality food to food banks across the country through a food diversion program' that paired retail stores with local food banks.[9] In Australia, the supermarket giant Woolworths established a partnership with the food rescue organization OzHarvest to divert food that would otherwise be wasted. Woolworth hopes by the year 2020 to stop any food from its stores being sent to landfills.

A few supermarkets have begun processing inedible food waste into energy via high-tech composting. Whole Foods and Stop & Shop markets in the United States have created programmes to send spoiled food to farms, where it is mixed with manure and piped into anaerobic digesters that break down biodegradable material to produce biogas that can be used to generate electricity.

Some supermarkets have created in-shop displays that offer customers food nearing its expiration date at a discount. Smartphone apps permit shoppers to order food nearing its expiration date and pick up their discounted purchases later. Tesco, the UK's biggest supermarket chain, established dedicated storage areas called 'Colleague Shops', which offer employees 'reduced-to-clear' food items as they approach their expiration date. Tesco also sends some unsold bread products to food-distribution charities and it converts some into a range of products, such as olive crostini and bread puddings.

Apps and Platforms

Supermarkets promote their waste-reduction programmes through a variety of media. Some feature unusually shaped produce, such as three-legged carrots, and stress that these products are discounted. Other chains hire 'anti-waste coaches' to advise them on how to prevent food waste. Some grocery chains now use apps to help distribute food to food-rescue organizations: FoodCloud 'links up local homeless shelters and food banks with about 740 stores across Britain and Ireland'.[10] Asda introduced the Surplus Swap app, which connects suppliers of surplus or unwanted food with others who can make use of it; app users upload images of what they can offer and any interested recipient can arrange to buy it.

Many chains now offer preferred customers lower prices on food nearing 'best by' dates. Walmart's Customer Value Program reduces the price on items that will soon expire.

The MyFoody app alerts residents of Milan, Italy, when food nearing the end of its shelf life is being offered at reduced prices in small local markets. It also offers home delivery services. In France, Zéro-gâchis (Zero-Waste) provides supermarkets with an efficient way to apply discounts on food items that are close to their sell-by dates. Food Rescue, an app collaboratively developed by Google and Sainsbury's, supplies recipes to help customers use up leftovers in their home kitchens. FoodLoop in Cologne, Germany, allows retail stores to sell short-dated foods by adjusting prices and targeting likely consumers.

Coop Danmark A/S, Denmark's largest supermarket chain, and Canada's Farm Boy Inc., a fresh food retailer in Ontario, have adopted an integrated retail and supply-chain planning programme called REFLEX, which tracks sell-by and use-by dates and forecasts sales and promotions, seasonal variations, weather and other factors to improve inventory management for perishable produce and decrease food spoilage. An Israeli start-up, Wasteless, sells a platform that automates pricing processes to reduce prices and incentivize sales of soon-to-expire produce and other store products and it informs managers of the need to reorder items when stock is low.

The Tokyo Metropolitan Government, in cooperation with NTT Docomo, Japan's largest mobile carrier, test-marketed a programme called 'EcoBuy' in 2018. Participating supermarkets discount food items approaching their 'best before' or 'consume by' dates and identify them with 'EcoBuy' stickers. Customers who participate in Docomo's membership programme upload images of receipts and product expiration dates onto their EcoBuy app and earn about 20 per cent of the original purchase price of products with short expiration dates. The Tokyo government subsidizes the app, which also provides recipes for using the EcoBuy products.

Many chains now use artificial intelligence technology to track produce from farm to shelf so company managers can ship fruits and vegetables to the right retail location. For instance, Walmart uses its Eden Technology and others use San Francisco-based Afresh Technologies to help managers optimize stocking.

Loop, an online zero-waste shopping platform, was sponsored by consumer product companies and TerraCycle, a waste-management company. It was piloted in the UK and launched in Paris and New York in the spring of 2019. Minimally packaged goods are delivered to homes in tote bags, and consumers collect packages and food waste in the totes for pickup by TerraCycle. All recovered waste is reused or recycled.

Governmental Actions

Voluntary action, public relations announcements and new apps are all helpful in reducing food waste, but more efforts are needed. Some countries have passed legislation to encourage or require retailers to reduce food waste. Japan began enacting laws in 2001 to promote recycling efforts, with supermarket chains such as Ito-Yokado, Seiyu, Uny and Aeon developing programmes that apply the '3 R's' (reduce, reuse and recycle) to create food-recycling loops. These loops typically convert unsold and uneaten food into fertilizer and animal feed which are in turn used to grow crops and raise fish that are then sold to the supermarket chains. In Europe Belgium passed a law requiring supermarkets to donate unsold products to local charities and food banks; supermarkets that donate to nine food banks registered by the Belgian Food Bank Federation receive a tax break.

The French ministries of Agriculture and the Environment issued a report in 2015, 'Fighting Food Waste: Proposals for a Public Policy', which recommended banning supermarkets from throwing away edible excess food or food that was usable as animal feed. A bill was introduced to levy fines on large supermarkets that deliberately spoiled or discarded edible food. The law, which was passed in 2016 and went into effect later that year, also banned expiration dates for certain products, such as wine and vinegar, and gave supermarket chains tax deductions for their donations. It also established educational programmes to teach primary school children about food waste. Some retailers found the law restrictive and unfair, pointing out that food waste occurred at all levels of distribution while the restrictions applied only to retailers.

France's passage of this law encouraged other European nations to consider similar legislation. Italian supermarkets that tried to donate food to charities had become entangled in red tape, and in August 2016 the government passed legislation removing obstacles and encouraging retailers to donate edible food slightly past its sell-by date. It created tax incentives for supermarkets and other retailers to donate unsold food to local charities and food banks. Unlike the French law, which penalizes those who fail to comply, the Italian legislation focuses on incentives, making it easier for grocery stores and supermarkets to decrease waste. Giving surplus food and food approaching its expiration date to food banks is a win–win–win situation for supermarkets: they don't have to pay for disposal, many receive a tax break for their donation and chains acquire positive public relations benefits for feeding the needy and saving the planet at the same time.

Most food-recovery programmes – and those they serve – are grateful to receive food that is near or past its 'best by' date. But some hunger advocates have complained that it is undignified for recipients. They also object that many of the donated foods are high in fat, salt and sugar and low in nutritional benefits. Rather than giving businesses tax breaks for these types of donations, some have argued that the food-distribution system must be redesigned to give everyone dignified access to healthful food. Yet few critics have offered practical solutions for creating such a system.

Zero-waste Stores and Anti-supermarkets

In the 1990s environmentalists called for 'precycling', the concept of eliminating rubbish before it is created. While precycling has yet to catch on in any substantial way, food co-ops in the U.S. and similar operations in other countries have sold some foods in bulk without packaging, for decades.

During the past fifteen years, zero-waste grocery stores have emerged, where customers bring their own containers and bags to refill, or the shop offers returnable containers or paper bags. These shops eliminate the massive amounts of plastic and other food packaging that ends up in landfill.

Zero-waste shops attract thrifty shoppers as well as environmentally minded ones. These are small operations that typically offer package-free and plastic-free bulk goods, including grains, produce and other products. Robuust, in Antwerp, Belgium, describes itself as a 'local speciality shop for organic, seasonal, and waste-free food'. Such shops typically encourage customers to bring their own reusable bags, jars or containers, and some offer reusable or compostable containers for sale or rent. Examples of waste-free markets include Negozio Leggero (Shop Light) in Sicily, En Vrac (In Bulk) in France, Lunzers Maß-Greißlerei (Bulk Grocery) in Austria, Shop Zero in South Africa, Original Unverpackt (Original Unpacked) in Berlin, The Hive Bulk in Malaysia, Granel (meaning 'bulk' in Catalan) in Barcelona and In.gredients in East Austin, Texas – to name just a few.

Zero-waste shops have generated widespread public interest. It is not just the lack of packaging that attracts customers: many products are sold at discounts of up to 40 per cent cheaper than traditional grocery stores. Waste-free shops do have limitations: they are small when compared with supermarkets and there are fewer products to choose from. Some food items cannot be sold loose because of public health laws. Some shops do not sell meat and they cannot sell products that are 'controlled designation of origin' or 'protected designation of origin' (such as certain olive oils and cheeses) due to the potential for fraud when they are removed from their original packages.

Waste generated by supermarket chains has encouraged the creation of 'anti-supermarkets' – shops that sell surplus

food or packaged goods discarded by supermarkets at substantial discounts (or give it away for free). Wastecooking,
an Austrian anti-food-waste group, opened Europe's first
free supermarket in Vienna in September 2012. It gave
away food rescued from the garbage, offered dumpster
diving and sponsored free cooking classes. In February
2016 Wefood, a food-rescue supermarket, opened in
Copenhagen, and a second branch opened later that year.
Volunteers collect surplus food from føtex and Dansk
Supermarked Group, two large food retailers, and from
other suppliers. The products are then offered for sale
in the Wefood stores at discounts of 30 to 50 per cent.
DanChurchAid, a charitable organization, uses the profits
to help fund its aid efforts around the world.

Similar 'anti-supermarkets' or free supermarkets have
opened in other countries. In the UK, HISBE opened in
Brighton in 2010, announcing that it was 'a rebellious
independent supermarket' that was environmentally friendly.
It has plastic-free aisles and refill stations. The staff do not
toss out any edible food. They avoid packaged foods and
encourage customers to bring their own containers. (But
HISBE does provide 'lovely compostable alternatives' if the
customer needs them.) In Dorchester, Massachusetts, the
Daily Table, a non-profit retail grocery store, sells food
that would have been thrown out by other shops due to
expiration dates or cosmetic flaws on fruit and vegetables.
Its 'meals are priced to compete with fast food options,
making it easier for families to eat healthier within their
means'.[11] The Good Food, Germany's first supermarket selling
only salvaged food, was opened in Cologne in February 2017.

Others have opened 'pay as you feel' shops, where there are no set prices and customers make donations for the food they acquire. The Real Junk Food Project (TRJFP) created a 'pay as you feel' supermarket in Pudsey, near Leeds, in September 2016.[12] Hong Kong's Green Price makes the rounds of retailers to collect food nearing its best-before date, then distributes them to low-income families. It has no fixed prices; customers pay what they believe the products are worth. In Tokyo, Share Mind, a non-profit that opened in September 2017, is an 'all free' recovered-food supermarket that feeds the needy. Pay-as-you-wish or low-cost grocery shops are continuing to open in other countries.

Committed to Reducing Food Waste

Supermarket chains throughout the world have taken steps to reduce food waste and plan to further reduce or eliminate waste in the future. In Japan, the Aeon Group has announced a programme that would cut food waste in half by 2025. Several UK supermarket chains have jointly committed to reducing the resources needed to provide food and drink by 20 per cent by the year 2025.[13] Asda has committed to a 'zero waste to landfill' policy by 2025 and is working towards 100 per cent renewable energy for its operations. Sainsbury's reported that it had achieved its goal of sending zero waste to landfills and that the company had developed 'more than 1,000 food donation partnerships with local charities'.[14] By June 2019, all major UK supermarket chains – and many other food-related businesses – had pledged to halve food waste by 2030, although precisely what that means and how waste will be calculated remains unclear.[15]

American supermarket chains have reported progress. Kroger, one of the largest U.S. grocery chains, created the 'Perishable Donations Partnership' and in 2015 sent 25 million kilograms (56 million lb) of fresh food to local food banks. By 2016, 32 of Kroger's distribution centres produced zero waste. The company's Zero Hunger Zero Waste plan is committed to eliminating hunger by 2025 in the communities where its 2,800 shops are located. Kroger has created an innovation fund for food-waste solutions. A Giant Food supermarket in Carlisle, Pennsylvania, engaged store employees and customers in an effort to reduce food waste. It succeeded in diverting 90 per cent of its waste from landfill or incineration. The U.S. Environmental Protection Agency designated it as one of America's first 'zero-waste' supermarkets.

Jumping on board the food-reduction programmes are Ahold USA, Delhaize America, Walmart, Wegmans Food Markets and Weis Markets. These chains have pledged,

> to reduce food loss and waste in their operations by 50 per cent by 2030 through activities aimed at preventing food from being lost or wasted in the first place, recovering still-good, otherwise wasted food for donation; and ensuring food that's lost or wasted can be recycled as animal feed or compost or used for energy generation.[16]

Walmart, the world's largest supermarket chain, recently installed an order-to-shelf (OTS) programme in some stores.

OTS sets strict standards for purchasing, storing and displaying products on shelves and in back rooms. In this system, employees can bypass stock rooms and move products directly from delivery trucks to shop shelves. This system has reduced spoilage, cut costs and cleared out storage areas, but it can also leave shelves partially or totally empty, which irritates customers. Another drawback is that some employees are mired in OTS-related paperwork to record deliveries. Still, environmentalists have hailed the system as a way to reduce food waste.

The Consumer Goods Forum (CGF) urged food manufacturers and retailers to reduce food waste from their operations by 50 per cent by 2025. To help measure progress, the World Resources Institute, in conjunction with the CGF and other organizations, developed a 'Food Loss and Waste Accounting and Reporting Standard' to track progress towards this goal.

One major problem with supermarket reports has been the lack of transparency about how chains define and measure food waste. UK supermarket chains have agreed on a common methodology to measure food waste and agreed to publish data on how much of it they generate each year. This means that company-specific data will be available and comparable among different businesses. Anti-food-waste advocates hope that the general public will also have access to this information.

5
RESTAURANT WASTE

Professional cooks are trained to waste nothing, but during the past few decades the amount of food discarded by restaurants and commercial kitchens has grown exponentially. A primary cause for this is the decline in food prices. Inexpensive ingredients removed the financial incentive for cooks and restaurant managers to conserve food. When food is cheap, there is no reason to save scraps, peels, mistakes and leftovers. Careless ordering, slipshod planning and the unpredictable vagaries of customer demand also lead to surplus food, both raw and prepared, that is all too easy to discard. Restaurant food waste initially became a public concern when people complained (and health inspectors took notice) of nauseating odours emanating from overflowing, vermin-infested bins found behind restaurants and other food-service operations.

Massive increases in waste also occur in large food-service operations, such as schools, hospitals, universities, company cafeterias, and cruise ships. Some institutional food-service programmes assemble trays in advance and serve food on a schedule regardless of the preferences or appetite of the people being fed. This results in vast quantities of food waste as patients, students and others refuse to eat what has been given to them.

Until the war on food waste gained visibility, reducing waste was a low priority for most restaurants. According to the non-profit Green Restaurant Association, North American restaurants each generate 11,000–34,000 kilograms (25,000–75,000 lb) of food waste annually, and two-thirds of that waste could have been avoided. Jonathan Bloom, author of *American Wasteland* (2011), estimated that for every restaurant meal served, about a half-pound (225 g) of food waste was created.

Food service waste increased substantially during the last decades of the twentieth century. In the television series *Ramsay's Kitchen Nightmares*, which first aired in 2004, chef Gordon Ramsay revealed the surprising scale of back-of-house waste. Ramsay visited failing restaurants, examined their operations and recommended improvements. During his review he sometimes rifled through the rubbish bins and complained about what the cooks were tossing out. (That said, he also threw out plenty of cooked food if it didn't meet his standards.) When Ramsay revisited the restaurants a few months later, he found that virtually all of them had decreased the amount of wasted food.

Waste Less, Save Money

u.s. retailers and food manufacturers created the Food Waste Reduction Alliance (FWRA) to develop a better understanding of food waste. An FWRA-sponsored report revealed that food-service operations accounted for a total of 42 per

cent of the nation's food waste. It broke down this figure
into three categories: full-service restaurants accounted for
19 per cent; fast-food restaurants contributed 13 per cent;
and institutional food-service operations (prisons, schools,
hospitals, and so on) contributed 11 per cent of the food
waste in the u.s.[1] Another FWRA survey found that 84.3 per
cent of unused food discarded by u.s. restaurants ended up
in landfills or incinerators; 14.3 per cent was recycled, mainly
via composting; and just 1.4 per cent was donated.[2]

Reduction of waste has become a major cause for the
food-service industry in the United States and around the
world. Chefs and managers play crucial roles in reducing
waste in their operations, but the realities of running a restaurant require them to make trade-offs in terms of portion
sizes, quality of food, kitchen procedures and menu options.
Inefficient operating and ordering procedures produce waste.
Then there is the inevitability of waste at the front of the
house, where customers leave food on their plates.

An estimated 4 to 10 per cent of food purchased by restaurants becomes waste before reaching the consumer.[3] A major
source of back-of-house waste is poor planning. Managers
order too much of a perishable product, and the surplus
is thrown out when it begins to spoil. (Better training in
food-safety protocols would help solve this problem.) Waste
also occurs in the process of preparation. Fruit and vegetable
peels are discarded, as are meat trimmings, and improperly
cooked food goes in the garbage, too. If restaurants reduced
the amount of food wasted, they could increase donations
of wholesome, nutritious food to those in need. Yet in the
United States only 2 per cent of restaurants say they donate

their surplus to food banks. One reason is that many agencies have a 'minimum pound requirement' for food pickups.

Food-service operations have reduced waste by implementing several procedures. First, managers need to predict their requirements for raw materials more accurately by studying existing sales patterns. Staff must be trained to gauge how much food to thaw, prepare and cook. They must be educated about safe temperatures and times for holding food in order to maintain quality, safety and freshness. Reducing waste makes financial sense and can even be profitable. It also makes sense from a legal standpoint, since in some localities it is now against the law for restaurants and food-service operations to send food waste to landfill.

Champions 12.3, a coalition of executives from governments, businesses, international organizations, research institutions and civil society, analysed the waste streams of 114 restaurants in twelve countries. They found that during the first year, restaurants that implemented food-saving measures reduced food waste by 26 per cent. Over a three-year period, benefit–cost ratio was $7 saved for every dollar spent implementing these measures.[4]

Reducing Plate Waste

Beginning in the 1950s, cheaper food and higher wages fuelled a surge in dining out. Whether driving up to a fast-food outlet or sitting down in a fine restaurant, people were eating more of their meals away from home. By the twenty-first century, money spent on food prepared outside the home approached 50 per cent of the total family food bills in some countries.

As more restaurant chains emerged to meet this opportunity, competition demanded that they offer special deals to attract customers in a crowded field. One very wasteful component of the food-service industry is the 'all-you-can-eat' buffet that is common in hotel dining rooms, particularly at breakfast. Cafeteria-style restaurants that serve buffets throughout the day and evening also discard large quantities of food. Displays are frequently overstocked to create the appearance of abundance. Customers fill their own plates, and since items are not individually priced they tend to take more than they can eat. Serving dishes are replenished as they are emptied to keep the buffet looking fresh and appealing. A recent study of hotel breakfast buffets found that nearly 50 per cent of the food served was wasted. This scene of abundance inevitably resulted in more food being left on those plates, destined for the bin. Fast-food chains came up with 'supersizing' – offering bigger burgers with double the usual amount of fries and huge drinks. Customers can't resist the deal, but many don't finish the meal, either, leading to even more waste. Today, chains are reluctant to change policies, which are often tied to the company's brand identity.

Once food has been served in a restaurant, the uneaten portion cannot be given to others due to health regulations and safety issues. Precisely how much food is left on diners' plates varies from country to country and from restaurant to restaurant. Studies indicate that restaurant patrons leave 11 to 17 per cent of their meals uneaten, and 55 per cent of these potential leftovers are not taken home.[5] Some restaurateurs compost this waste or convert it into biogas, but most waste is sent to landfill or incinerators.

Restaurateurs have come up with ways of reducing the waste that comes with excessive portions. One is simply to serve less – putting the food on a smaller plate helps disguise the downsizing. Another solution is to offer a range of portion sizes. Some restaurants offer half-portions, such as half a sandwich with a cup of soup for lunch. A very creative approach was initiated in 2012 by the Stop Hunger programme in São Paulo, Brazil. Its 'Satisfeito' (satisfied) programme designed icons to be placed next to items on a restaurant menu. Customers choosing the Satisfeito version are served one-third less but are charged full price. The resulting savings are donated by the restaurant to organizations that fight child hunger, and customers seem to appreciate that: by 2016, more than sixty restaurants participated in the initiative, most in São Paulo, but also in other Brazilian cities, Mexico and South Africa.

A crucial factor in reducing restaurant food waste is knowing which items diners are leaving uneaten. Front-of-house staff can record what is left on plates so that portion sizes of specific menu items can be reduced. In one such case it was discovered that placing a portion of vegetables on each plate, rather than bringing them to the table in a serving dish, reduced waste.

Doggy Bags

By far the most significant way to reduce customer waste at restaurants is to encourage diners to take home their leftovers in 'doggy bags'. The idea of the doggy bag originated in the United States after the Second World War. With the economy booming, Americans had extra money in their pockets and they were happy to spend it dining out. Customers who had enjoyed a meal but were unable to finish it began asking – with a wink – for a 'doggy bag' in which to carry home the leftovers. The food would more likely serve as a second meal than be given to the family pet, but the leftovers might well linger at the back of the refrigerator until they spoiled.

Health officials worried about the safety of the food in a doggy bag before it was brought home: room temperature is conducive to the growth of bacteria, which could result in food poisoning. Cooked food should be refrigerated within two hours and then reheated to a temperature above 75°C (167°F) before eating. But that doesn't always happen.

It took time for doggy bags to catch on outside the United States. Sociologist Jean-Pierre Corbeau at the University of Tours noted that in France both the upper and lower classes shunned the idea. For the upper class, leaving food on one's plate was a sign of affluence; for the working class, 'cleaning your plate' was mandatory. But by 2015 this had changed. A poll indicated that 75 per cent of people in France were willing to take uneaten food home from a restaurant – but this was not followed by a corresponding change in behaviour: asking for a doggy bag was still too embarrassing. To convince restaurant customers to take home their leftovers, officials in the great gastronomic city of Lyon tried to shine a more positive light on the practice. It replaced the term 'doggy bag' with *sac-à-emporter* (carry bag) or 'gourmet bag' and introduced the promotional tagline *c'est si bon, je finis à la maison* (it's so good, I'll finish it at home).[6] A bill to require large restaurants to offer 'le doggy bag' – or its officially sanctioned name, 'le gourmet bag' – to patrons was passed by the French parliament in 2016.

In the past, Italian diners might take home a steak bone for the dog, but rarely would they take food to eat themselves. But that was before restaurants began supplying doggy bags. Milano Ristorazione, a government organization that supplied meals to schools, hospitals and homes for the elderly, launched a campaign called *Io non spreco* (I don't waste), which gave bags to primary school students so they could take home leftover food from lunch. Italy passed a law directing restaurants to provide doggie bags, now renamed 'family bags', on request, and authorities have tried to encourage their use by promoting food-saving as a virtue.

Doggie bags were somewhat more common in the UK. The London-based Sustainable Restaurant Association announced a campaign to tackle 'plate waste' by supplying branded 'doggy boxes' to participating restaurants. In 2016 the Scottish government began providing free bags to restaurants, launching the 'Good to Go' campaign to encourage customers to take home leftovers. Studies indicated that doggie bags contributed to a 40 per cent reduction in food waste from participating restaurants in Scotland.

The German government created the 'Beste-Reste-Box' (best leftover box), a compostable folding carton with a handle, to encourage diners to pack up leftovers and take them home. The boxes are water- and grease-resistant; they can be stored in the freezer and leftovers can be microwaved right in the box. Beste-Reste-Boxes are recyclable and biodegradable.

Doggy bags, even if widely adopted, will not solve all front-of-house waste. Customers may not be headed home (or to a location with a refrigerator) after eating, and some just find doggy bags inconvenient and awkward to use. Others are embarrassed to ask for a doggy bag. In the meantime, a couple of restaurants have come up with another solution: they charge customers if they do not eat what they order or take home.

Zero-waste Restaurants and Cafés

The environmental movement rekindled interest in reusing, reducing and recycling waste in restaurants. Some reduced their use of water. Others decreased their energy use or converted to renewable energy sources such as solar or wind power. Still others installed new technology and redesigned their facilities to reduce the need for heating, cooling and lighting systems. There was a new focus on recycling paper, cardboard, glass and plastics, and composting food waste. Some restaurateurs began identifying their establishments as 'green' and by the 1990s certification programmes, such as that offered by the Green Restaurant Association, identified restaurants, cafés and bars as 'zero-waste' or 'near zero-waste' when they reduced their total waste by 90 per cent.[7]

Today, zero-waste or near-zero-waste restaurants, cafés, pubs and bars are operating in many cities. Chicago's Sandwich Me In, a fast-food eatery that opened in 2012, operated on sustainable energy; its food came minimally packaged from local farms and was then served to customers in modest wrapping. The goal was to recycle, reuse or repurpose everything. The main waste was coffee cups, newspapers and other material left behind by customers. Another zero-waste operation, Hannah's Bretzel, was started by German-born Florian Pfahle. Its four shops in downtown Chicago run on wind and solar power and they compost all leftovers.

Zero-waste restaurants also began to appear in the UK. The first was Silo in Brighton, opened by chef Douglas McMaster in 2014. Products are delivered to the restaurant in reusable crates, cans, pails and urns. Leftover food is fed to 'Bertha', an aerobic digester, which generates compost. McMaster also started the Old Tree Brewery, which produces alcoholic beverages using foraged and surplus plants, herbs, vegetables and fruit. His catchphrase is, 'Waste is a failure of imagination.' The Tiny Leaf, an organic, vegetarian, zero-waste restaurant, opened temporarily in 2016 at Mercato Metropolitano, an Italian street-food market in London. It served affordable meals made from surplus food supplied by organic wholesalers, supermarkets, farms, distributors and other retailers. At the Arbor Restaurant on the southern coast of England, chef Andy Hilton turns the majority of the surplus produce into tasty dishes. Bartender Ryan Chetiyawardana, famous for his invention of waste-free cocktails, opened Cub in Hoxton, London, where every dish and cocktail 'centres around a single ingredient and [is] conceived to minimise waste'.[8]

Low- or zero-waste restaurants also opened in other countries. In Malleswaram, India, the New Krishna Bhavan restaurant was opened by Gopinath Prabhu in 2013. Unable to locate a reliable waste-collection service, he set out to make his restaurant a zero-waste operation. Wet waste is sent to a piggery and dry waste is given to rag-pickers who earn money selling it for recycling. Coffee grounds and used tea leaves are composted and used as fertilizer at a nearby park, and coconut shells are sold to a rope maker. Toronto's Maizal Quesadilla Café is a Mexican-style restaurant that maintains a zero food-waste policy. Once a week all food waste is trucked to Cavaleiro Farms in nearby Schomberg, where it is fed to pigs or composted. The driver picks up fresh produce at the farm and delivers it to the restaurant on the return trip. In Glasgow, Scotland, Brew Box Coffee opened in 2016. This micro café is situated in a Tardis – a replica of a structure that appears in the *Doctor Who* television series. All packaging is biodegradable, as are the coffee pods, and all waste is composted.

Instock started as a pop-up restaurant in Amsterdam in 2014. Ingredients were sourced from vendors who had an unsold surplus of food or drinks. Instock became a non-profit operation and opened additional locations in Utrecht and The Hague. Based on their experiences preparing food at Instock, Brigitta Gadellaa and the chef Lucas Jeffries wrote *Instock cooking: zet voedselverspilling op de kaart* (Instock Cooking: Put Food Waste On the Map), a cookbook with recipes and preservation techniques such as sweet and sour pickling, sugaring, bottling, fermenting, drying, freezing, brining and smoking.

Chef Jehangir Mehta created a nearly zero-waste restaurant, Graffiti Earth, in New York City. Mehta's approach, inspired by his Persian and Indian background, is to look at each ingredient – right down to the scraps – as a new source of inspiration. Some of his menu items include vegetable soup made entirely from salvaged produce and a sweet and savoury scallop brûlée made with broken diver scallops that are otherwise unsaleable. He uses the BlueCart app, an industry resource-management app, to streamline his ordering and further reduce waste. Other chefs who have created 'zero-waste kitchens' include Tanya Holland of Brown Sugar Kitchen in Oakland, California, and Clayton Chapman of The Grey Plume in Omaha, Nebraska.

Dutch-born Joost Bakker opened Brothl, a soup eatery, in Melbourne, Australia, in 2012, using food waste from high-end restaurants to make the broth. Brothl was closed in 2015 by the city council due to a dispute about the establishment's compost machine. One of Brothl's chefs, Matt Stone, went on to become head chef of the Oakridge winery in Victoria, and to co-star in the National Geographic television show *Recipes That Rock*. His recipes were published in his book *The Natural Cook: Maximum Taste, Zero Waste* (2016).

Other zero-waste or eco-friendly service operations around the world include Café Isla in Berlin; Lupii Café in Vancouver; Lemonjello's Coffee in Holland, Michigan; BioM in Copenhagen; and Maaemo in Oslo, Norway.

Nose-to-Tail to Root-to-Leaf Dining

While some restaurateurs were improving their sustainability index, many chefs began to repurpose food that would otherwise be thrown out by restaurants, farmers, food processors and food retailers. Fergus Henderson caused a sensation when he opened his London restaurant, St John, in 1995, offering 'nose-to-tail' dishes that used every part of the animal, especially those rarely served in restaurants. He popularized this philosophy in the book *Nose to Tail Eating: A Kind of British Cooking* (1999). Henderson's signature dishes include roast bone marrow and parsley salad, pig's trotters stuffed with potato, and fennel and ox-tongue soup. Nose-to-tail cookery took off in the early twenty-first century and hundreds of restaurants and chefs proudly proclaimed that they used every bit of the animal, including the internal organs (also known as 'variety meats' or offal).

Noma, the world-renowned Copenhagen restaurant, was co-founded by the chefs René Redzepi and Mads Refslund in 2003. Both are expert foragers who are dedicated to using wild foods in their dishes; the kitchen also salvages scraps of vegetables and fruits and animal parts that would normally go to waste. Redzepi implemented a zero-waste compost system capable of reducing food waste by up to 90 per cent. Refslund, with professional forager Tama Matsuoka Wong, published *Scraps, Wilt and Weeds: Turning Wasted Food into Plenty* in 2017. Recipes include Carrot Tops Pesto, Roasted Cauliflower Stalks with Mushrooms and Brie, Crispy Salmon Skin Puffs with Horseradish-buttermilk Dip, Pork Ribs Glazed with Overripe Pear Sauce, and Beer and Bread Porridge with Salted Caramel Ice Cream.

April Bloomfield, the British-born chef at the New York gastropub The Spotted Pig, authored *A Girl and Her Pig: Recipes and Stories* (2012), which promoted nose-to-tail cuisine. The chef and restaurateur Andrew Fairlie in Perthshire, Scotland, is another proponent of using the whole animal, but he scoffs at the idea that it's a new trend. 'It's cost effective. Buying local? Using the whole beast? It drives me mad when people boast about these things. Any self-respecting chef should be buying local and using as much of the animal as possible.'[9]

Nose-to-tail eating fostered the development of 'root-to-stalk' or 'root-to-leaf' cooking – using every part of vegetables and fruits that were typically removed and discarded, such as green leek tops, broccoli and cauliflower stems, turnip and carrot greens, cabbage cores, potato peels, melon rinds and pea pods. Tara Duggan's *Root to Stalk Cooking: The Art of Using the Whole Vegetable* (2013) and Steven Satterfield's *Root to Leaf: A Southern Chef Cooks through the Seasons* (2015) popularized the idea, as did April Bloomfield's second cookbook, *A Girl and Her Greens: Hearty Meals from the Garden* (2015). Tom Hunt, author of *The Natural Cook: Eating the Seasons from Root to Fruit* (2016) and owner of Poco in Bristol, espouses a 'root to fruit' culinary philosophy. It turns 'uneaten extras into other delicious meals', ensuring that absolutely all vegetable scraps and skins are used.

It isn't just high-end restaurants that have adopted nose-to-tail items. Dishes made with pigs' ears, pork bellies, calf brains, chicken feet, tripe, tongue, hearts and other less commonly used products are relatively inexpensive to make. Chefs have found that if they prepare these ingredients thoughtfully and price them modestly, they'll be well received by customers. Whether these out-of-the-box dishes and recipes are just attention-getters, or they are intended for more altruistic reasons, chefs and restaurateurs have reduced food waste and have helped customers and readers understand the need for saving food.

PAYF Cafés

In 2000, Sri Lankan-born Shanaka Fernando founded
Lentil As Anything, a non-profit vegetarian restaurant in
Melbourne, Australia (its name was a play on the Australian
band 'Mental As Anything'). It had no posted prices and
no cash register, and anyone who wanted a meal could eat
on a 'pay as you feel' (PAYF) basis. It was such a success that
Fernando opened locations in other Australian cities. In
his autobiography, *Lentil as Anything: Everybody Deserves
a Place at the Table* (2012), Fernando hoped that PAYF cafés
would serve as an antidote to the 'hubris, greed and heedless-
ness' that had shaken the world during the global financial
crisis that began in 2008.[10]

Adam Smith, a UK-born chef living in Melbourne at the
time, was impressed with the Lentil As Anything operation.
He had observed the vast amount of edible food that other
restaurants sent to landfill. When he returned to England
in 2013, he combined these two concepts in a PAYF café in
Leeds. Unlike those in Australia, Smith's café used surplus
groceries donated by food-service businesses, transforming
them into restaurant-quality meals. The following year he
launched The Real Junk Food Project (TRJFP), a non-profit
organization staffed by volunteers, which opened additional
PAYF cafés in other communities. By 2017 TRJFP was running
more than 120 cafés and shops in seven countries, including
Australia, Israel and the United States.

PAYF cafés have opened in many other cities. In
Aberystwyth, Wales, the PAYF café at St Paul's Methodist
Church is run by volunteers, who prepare and serve a

vegetarian lunch for those in need. Amsterdam's Trust Lunchroom acquires ingredients from a local market and serves waste-free vegetarian meals. In Madison, Wisconsin, Little John's takes excess food and turns out affordable, chef-quality meals. Many PAYF cafés are pop-ups – and many have a limited lifespan. Everybody Eats in Auckland, New Zealand, however, was launched as a pop-up, but converted into a permanent PAYF café in 2018.

Apps, Platforms and Services

A number of management systems have been developed to help food-service businesses reduce waste, and consulting firms have emerged to assist large food-service operations in food-waste reduction efforts. Wise Up On Waste, an app developed for Unilever, helps professional kitchens monitor and track food waste. It identifies when and where food waste is generated and identifies potential cost saving if waste is reduced. U.S.-based LeanPath has worked with more than 150 food-service operations in eleven countries since its founding in 2004. Kitchens that implement LeanPath claim to have prevented more than 11 million kilograms (25 million lb) of food from being wasted since 2014. London-based Winnow Systems, a UK start-up formed in 2013, has developed a 'smart meter' that helps commercial kitchens identify, measure and analyse food waste. It totals the value of the waste, then compiles weekly reports to identify the financial cost of the waste and how it could be reduced. By November 2017, Winnow claimed that its systems had turned waste into the equivalent of 350,000 meals in commercial kitchens in Australia,

Europe and the United States. Major food-service businesses including IKEA, Compass Group and Accor Hotels claimed that Winnow had reduced their food waste by 50 per cent within twelve months.[11] Other platforms and apps identify cost savings, improve efficiency and track and monitor food waste in restaurants. These include MintScraps (Washington, DC), OrderPoint Solutions (Ireland), SimpleOrder (Tel Aviv) and Kitchen CUT (U.S.-based).

By implementing the recommendations made by these and other platforms, restaurants and food-service operations can digitize and streamline their workings, from purchasing and managing suppliers to inventory tracking. Some of the systems even supply information on the cost of specific recipes. These have the potential to substantially reduce waste, uncover savings and support sustainability initiatives. The Food Waste Management Cost Calculator app, sponsored by the U.S. Environmental Protection Agency, estimates the cost competitiveness of alternatives to food-waste disposal, including source reduction, donation, composting and grease recycling.

Still other platforms help food-service operations find ways to donate surplus food that would otherwise go to waste. ChowMatch is a software technology that connects restaurants, grocery stores, caterers and farmers with food banks, family shelters and other food-recovery organizations. By 2019 ChowMatch operated in more than five hundred cities and towns. Rescuing Leftover Cuisine in Massachusetts, and Zero Percent in Chicago, are apps that alert volunteers when restaurants, offices and events have unserved food so that it can be ferried to homeless shelters.

Similar programmes have emerged in other states. Likewise, the app Copia Connect helps companies with large inventories manage and find non-profits to donate excess food to. It also enables these businesses to receive a tax write-off and reduce disposal costs.

Large food-service operations have started waste-reduction programmes. IKEA, the Swedish furniture retailer that also runs one of the world's largest restaurant chains, began the 'Food is Precious' campaign in December 2016. It targeted food waste in twenty of its kitchens and food-service operations. Bon Appétit Management Company, which operates more than 650 cafés in the U.S., developed Imperfectly Delicious Produce, a programme intended to rescue 'cosmetically challenged' produce for use in its own businesses.

Hotels, hospitals and airports have also embarked on programmes to reduce food waste. The World Wildlife Fund began a partnership in 2015 with the Hilton hotel chain to explore the issues of food waste, sustainable seafood and ocean stewardship. The American Hotel & Lodging Association (AHLA) discovered a desperate need for industry-wide training and education on food-waste reduction among hotel properties, finding a general lack of measurement and tracking of food waste. The AHLA recommended creating menus designed to limit food waste and raising awareness among hotel guests. The Pacific Asia Tourist Association sponsored BUFFET (Building an Understanding For Food Excess in Tourism), a campaign to help hospitality operations in Asia and the Pacific reduce food waste.

High-profile Events

Celebrity chefs often garner more media attention than social activists, and for two decades they have publicized the urgent need for food recovery and food-waste reduction through high-profile events. One of the first of these was organized by anti-food-waste activist Tristram Stuart. He and others hosted a 'Feeding the 5000' event in 2009 that used surplus and discarded food to feed thousands for free in London's Trafalgar Square. Since then, more than forty such events have been organized in cities around the world. At each of these, local celebrity chefs, using salvaged food, prepare meals for crowds of attendees. These efforts educate people about food-waste issues while providing them with a good meal. They have helped catalyse food-recovery efforts and promoted a wide range of innovative solutions to the food-waste crisis. 'Feeding the 5000' events also give participating chefs good visibility, inspiring their peers to join the movement and organize their own events.

In the Fläming Heath region of Germany, the Dutch chef-activist Wam Kat founded the Fläming Kitchen, a mobile operation that could serve up to 5,000 people vegan or vegetarian hot meals. Beginning in 2012, the Fläming Kitchen began to hold anti-food-waste events called 'Schnippeldiskos' (Disco Soup) – gatherings of volunteers who joined forces to make massive pots of soup from produce that would otherwise have been tossed out. The soup was served to thousands of people who participated in 'Wir haben es satt!' (We Are Fed Up!) events run by Slow Food Youth in Germany. As Stuart explained it, 'Disco Soup is a culinary and community experience that involves gathering, sourcing, cooking and celebrating food. Everyone has the power – and the responsibility – to help solve the global food waste scandal and join the food waste movement'.[12] Disco Soup days have been celebrated in dozens of countries around the world. The Slow Food Youth Network designated 28 April 'World Disco Soup Day'.

Dan Barber, the chef/owner of Blue Hill restaurant in New York City, is a proponent of 'nose-to-tail, root-to-stem' dining. Barber put aside his upscale farm-to-table menu and opened a three-week pop-up called 'wastED' at Blue Hill. A rotation of twenty top chefs, including Danny Bowien, April Bloomfield, Mario Batali, Grant Achatz and Daniel Humm, cooked meals devoted to preventing waste and promoting food recovery. Their goal was to create delicious dishes using typically overlooked by-products from local farmers and purveyors. Offcuts from local butchers as well as vegetable pulp from a nearby juice shop were among the salvaged ingredients. Menu items included Dumpster Dive Vegetable Salad, Monkfish Wings, Cured Cuts of Waste-fed Pigs, Juice Pulp Cheeseburger and Double Whey Bread Pudding.

During President Barack Obama's second term, Barber teamed up with White House chef Sam Kass to create an eco-friendly meal for thirty world leaders, including the French president François Hollande and UN Secretary-General Ban Ki-moon. They served such delights as 'Landfill Salad' (made from vegetable scraps, and rejected apples and pears), veggie burgers (made from pulp leftover from juicing), buns (made from old bread) and 'cow-corn' French fries (made from the type of corn normally fed to cattle). Barber opened another pop-up on the rooftop of Selfridges, the iconic department store on London's Oxford Street. Chefs Isaac McHale, Gordon Ramsay, Yotam Ottolenghi, Alain Ducasse, Jean-Philippe Blondet and Fergus Henderson prepared dishes such as juice-pulp burgers, cod cheeks and collars, and a salt beef-ends burrito wrapped in a crêpe made from pig's blood and bran.

Other chefs have opened pop-ups focusing on reducing food waste. Australian-born Skye Gyngell, the executive chef at Spring restaurant in London, devised one called TABLE at Spring. The dishes were 'created from excess produce donated by partnering restaurants and farms'. TABLE showcased a three-course pre-theatre 'scratch menu' based on kitchen leftovers. During London Food Month in June 2017, Gyngell teamed up with Merlin Labron-Johnson, then the chef at London's Portland restaurant, to create a 'Spring X Portland Lunch', also based on food that traditionally would have been tossed out. The lunch was priced at £40 and the profits went to The Felix Project, a charity that collects surplus food from supermarkets and wholesalers and delivers it to charities that prepare nutritious meals for the hungry in London.

Cocktails are often garnished with bits of produce that customers put aside when they sip their drinks, so bars have been targeted as food-waste culprits. Some bartenders, however, have taken the food-waste issue to heart. Rich Woods, the mixologist at Duck & Waffle in London, developed cocktail recipes based on ingredients such as banana skins, tomato stalks and leaves, and asparagus butts.

He sponsored an 'Urban Foraging vs Urban Decay' menu featuring cocktails made with burnt toast, avocado peels and coffee grounds, and published the recipes for the drinks in *The Cocktail Guy: Infusions, Distillations and Innovative Combinations* (2017). At Providence, a restaurant in Los Angeles, bartender Kim Stodel started a zero-waste cocktail programme that turns kitchen scraps and fruit and vegetable peels into syrups, salts, sugars, oils, fruit leathers and liquor infusions. In Washington, DC, the mixologist Trevor Frye makes liquid garnishes from citrus peels infused with vodka, which are then sprayed onto cocktails just before they are served. London cocktail bartenders Iain Griffiths of White Lyan and Kelsey Ramage have reimagined cocktails through repurposing food. Among their ingredients are citrus peels, avocado pits and pineapple skin. Griffiths and Ramage have toured Asia, the U.S. and Canada demonstrating their skills at 'Trash Tiki' pop-ups.

Expo Milano opened in 2015 with the theme 'Feeding the Planet: Energy for Life'. Massimo Bottura, the chef/owner of Osteria Francescana (which was voted the best restaurant in the world in 2018), was invited to cook for various functions at the Expo. Together, he opened a soup kitchen called Refettorio Ambrosiano in a former church hall in a poor section of the city. He invited renowned chefs, including Mario Batali, Ferran Adrià, Daniel Patterson, Alain Ducasse, Daniel Humm, Gastón Acurio and René Redzepi, to prepare high-end meals for refugees, the homeless and the working poor using repurposed food waste from the Coop supermarket at the Expo. The Refettorio Ambrosiano was a tremendous success: it not only fed 96 guests every evening but generated priceless publicity for the importance of reducing food waste.

The Refettorio Ambrosiano was such a success that the chefs' recipes were published in Bottura's *Bread is Gold: Extraordinary Meals with Ordinary Ingredients* (2017). The National Film Board of Italy produced a documentary about the Refettorio Ambrosiano called *Theatre of Life*, which was released in 2016. It features chefs who had prepared food at the soup kitchen and includes interviews with six guests who dined there. When the film premiered in various cities, chefs were inspired to offer meals based on food that would otherwise have been wasted. For the film's opening gala in Vancouver, Canada, Robert Clarke of The Arbor restaurant and other chefs created and served dishes from rescued food, which they dubbed 'compost cuisine' – a phrase that, understandably, didn't catch on.

When Expo Milano ended, Refettorio Ambrosiano stayed open, run in conjunction with Caritas, an international food recovery charity that supports soup kitchens around the world. The Refettorio earned Bottura a grant from the Rockefeller Foundation and he started the non-profit organization Food for Soul, which aimed to empower communities to fight food waste by including everyone – not just the needy. Its first project was the Refettorio Gastromotiva, which was conducted with chef and social entrepreneur David Hertz at the Rio de Janeiro Olympics in the summer of 2016. Refettorio Gastromotiva transformed surplus food from the Olympic dining facilities into healthy meals for the working poor.

Food for Soul's next international project was the Refettorio Felix at St Cuthbert's Centre during London

Food Month in 2017, which involved Bottura along with more than fifty other top chefs. When asked about his interest in reducing food waste, Bottura's response was, 'We want to fight waste, or at least what other people think is waste – for us, it's just ingredients.'[13]

Francesco Mazzei, the chef/owner of several London restaurants, participated in Refettorio Felix and returned regularly to the soup kitchen at St Cuthbert's Centre to prepare food for the poor. His cookbook *Mezzogiorno: Southern Italian Cooking* (2015), explained how economic hardships faced in southern Italy shaped a cuisine that shunned waste and used ingredients thriftily. Mazzei also helped initiate a food waste campaign in his home town, Cerchiara di Calabria; during a festival he prepared a meal with ingredients such as bruised aubergines, overripe tomatoes and pigs' heads.

Chef Flicks and Television Series

Celebrity chefs emerged during the 1970s, thanks to popular cooking demonstration shows and, later, television programmes. Stardom gave chefs a bully pulpit to discuss issues and problems related to the food system. Food waste was a perfect issue to highlight on television and in films. Chefs showed home cooks how to avoid waste and save money; they also explained the negative consequences of food waste on the environment and raised awareness of programmes underway around the world to help feed the hungry and prevent waste.

Food waste was addressed on television programmes such as the aforementioned *Ramsay's Kitchen Nightmares* and Jamie Oliver and Jimmy Doherty's *Friday Night Feast* in the

2000s, but when the war on food waste commenced in 2009, food waste became a hot media topic around the world. BBC1 aired the documentary *The Great British Waste Menu* in 2010. It followed four chefs – Angela Hartnett, Richard Corrigan, Matt Tebbutt and Simon Rimmer – as they dug into Britain's food-waste problem. The chefs secured abundant supplies of unwanted food from supermarkets, markets, farms and homes, and then transformed the ingredients into mouth-watering dishes. The British chef and activist Hugh Fearnley-Whittingstall hosted the BBC series *Hugh's War on Waste* in January 2016. The first episodes investigated food waste in supermarkets and the fast-food industry and explored ways to drastically reduce the amount of waste they generate.

In America, the Food Network's *The Big Waste* featured four chefs – Bobby Flay, Michael Symon, Anne Burrell and Alex Guarnaschelli. They were split into two teams and given 48 hours to create a multi-course banquet using only food that was on its way to the bin. Gabrielle Hamilton, the chef/owner of Prune in New York City, offered many suggestions for repurposing food when she hosted a season of the PBS series *Mind of a Chef*. In the 'Garbage' episode, she demonstrated how delicious 'food waste' could be. Chef Anthony Bourdain's eco-documentary *Wasted! The Story of Food Waste* showcased celebrity chefs, such as Dan Barber, Mario Batali, Danny Bowien and Massimo Bottura, and profiled individuals and organizations engaged in food recovery around the world.

The Austrian activist David Gross, a trained chef, began dumpster diving in 2012 and peeked into rubbish bins marked for organic waste; he was shocked at how much edible food he found. He started Wastecooking, a collective that focused on reducing food waste, and in May 2012 he began filming his exploits foraging and preparing food he had rescued from garbage disposals. Two years later, Georg Misch filmed Gross as he journeyed through European countries gathering discarded food and preparing meals with it. His travelling kitchen was a converted waste receptacle that he towed behind a biodiesel-fuelled vehicle. This resulted in a five-part series, *Wastecooking: Kochen statt Verschwenden* (Wastecooking: Make Food, Not Waste), which first aired in 2015. The series was filmed in Salzburg, Vienna, Geneva and London, where chefs, scientists and activists presented simple solutions to the food-waste epidemic. The second season of *Wastecooking* explored food waste in Denmark, Great Britain, Italy, Greece and Romania.

Cheap Eats and More Apps

Restaurants and food-service operations prepare food based on sales predictions. Often, restaurants prepare more food than they are able to sell by closing time. Traditionally, employees were given any leftover food, and many restaurants continue this practice today. But recently another solution has emerged: apps that help restaurants sell surplus food near closing time or during slow periods of the day. Singapore's treatsure app permits merchants to offer their surplus food at a discount of 20 to 30 per cent online, usually towards the end of the day. Similar apps include the Food Savior (Hong Kong), Freshly (Malta) and Grub Cycle

(Malaysia); they list surplus food available at a discount from stores, restaurants and cafés.

Similar apps are available in many other countries. Toronto's Feedback and Flashfood apps cut down food waste by enabling users to buy restaurant meals destined for the bin at a fraction of the original price. The network also collects excess food from restaurants, caterers and conventions and delivers it to nearby community centres. The BuffetGO app in Scandinavia permits buffet restaurants to offer closing-time discounts so that less food ends up in the bin. Karma helps restaurants and cafés in many countries reduce their food waste by selling their surplus to consumers at drastically reduced prices at the end of breakfast, lunch or dinner services. By April 2019 it had an estimated half a million registered users. Similar apps, such as MealSaver, ResQ Club, Too Good To Go (TGTG), Food for All, GoMkt and Halfy Hour, are in use in other countries.

Other apps approach food waste in different ways. Food Connect Group started as Operation Food Rescue during the 2016 Democratic National Convention in Philadelphia. A collaborative effort by the city's leading anti-hunger organizations, it 'bridged the gap between surplus food and hunger by transporting excess food from large events and from restaurants in Philadelphia to area food banks, pantries and emergency meal providers'. The Atlanta-based Goodr Food Rescue app works like Lyft or Uber: event planners, restaurants, chefs, hotels, schools and even hospitals can have a driver collect surplus food and deliver it to soup kitchens, shelters, food pantries and families or individuals struggling with food poverty. Goodr uses blockchain technology to track surplus food, avoid miscommunications and record potential tax deductions for those donating surplus food.

In New York, for every order placed with the delivery app Sharebite, a meal is donated to a child in need. As of May 2019, more than 300,000 meals had been donated to City Harvest through Sharebite and thousands of dollars were given to non-profits. SnackPass, a smartphone app, permits subscribers to pick up five snacks from Chicago-area restaurants for a $10 monthly fee. The funds generated from SnackPass are used to transport surplus prepared and perishable food from restaurants and other retail food operations to neighbourhood charities.

6
CONSUMER WASTE

The virtue of minimizing food waste has been built into most cultures and religions throughout history, and for thousands of years homemakers have employed various techniques to help prevent food spoilage. Oral traditions emphasized the value of squandering nothing and learning ways to utilize every bit of edible food.

During the late nineteenth century, many new techniques were developed to preserve food for longer. These include improved food packaging, such as machine-made metal cans and glass bottles, and paper and cardboard boxes and bags. New processes, such as pasteurization and chlorination, helped keep food and beverages safer for longer periods of time. The advent of plastic packaging materials and the widespread adoption of freezers in supermarkets and homes in the decades after the Second World War increased the longevity of many foods, reducing the need to consume them soon after bringing them home. Despite these changes, food waste rapidly expanded during the second half of the twentieth century. In high-income countries, the weakest link in the food-waste chain is the consumer.

People waste food for many reasons, including inadequate planning before and during shopping; 'irresistible' bargains that lead to overbuying; failure to understand date labels on processed foods; ignorance of how to prepare and serve leftovers; self-consciousness about taking home uneaten food when dining out; improper storage of food; and general apathy about conserving and reusing leftovers. Perhaps one of the most significant reasons for consumer food waste is that people are stressed out and pressed for time: conserving leftovers is just not a priority. As a result, consumers throw out large amounts of perfectly edible food at home, at restaurants, in the workplace, at school and in public gathering places.

The easiest place to evaluate consumer waste is in the home. The average u.s. household, for instance, throws out 580 grams (1.28 lb) of food a day, which includes 20 per cent of the milk, 23 per cent of the eggs and 40 per cent of the fresh fish the family purchases. This does not include food that was ground down the garbage disposal, added to a compost heap or fed to family pets. A study conducted by the Johns Hopkins Center for a Livable Future concluded that about 1 billion kilograms (2.3 billion lb) of seafood – almost 50 per cent of America's processed seafood – ended up in the bin. In total, American consumers waste an estimated 589 million kilograms (1.3 billion lb) of food annually.[1]

The average American household wastes anywhere from $1,365 to $2,275 annually on food that goes uneaten.[2] Consumer food waste in other countries is also significant: Australian households throw out A$8–10 billion worth of food every year and lose an estimated A$3,800 per year by discarding food. Households in the UK waste an estimated 6.7 million tonnes of food, which means that annually about 32 per cent of all food purchased by consumers is not eaten, costing the average family £700.[3] Households in New Zealand waste NZ$563 worth of food a year.[4] Scottish households throw out enough food annually to make 800 million meals, which equals an estimated £460 per family per year.[5] In Israel, annual household food waste costs the average family about $890-worth in food per year, which equates to a month and a half's worth of food.[6] Irish households lose between €700 and €1,000 annually due to food waste.[7] However the numbers are crunched, families around the world forfeit considerable funds buying food that ends up in the trash.

Deskilling and Consumer Food Waste

Until the early twentieth century, most food was prepared in the home. Home cooks were skilled in salvaging uneaten food and working it into new dishes for the following meals. But social and culinary changes in the late twentieth century led to a decline in home cooking and an attendant loss of kitchen skills, such as inventive use of leftovers. And with more and more people living in cities, composting food waste or feeding it to animals were no longer options.

Social fabrics took on new patterns during the twentieth century. As middle-class women entered the workforce they had less time for shopping, cooking and eating sit-down meals. Feminists questioned domesticity in general and in particular the uncompensated housework that limited the time women could devote to their careers. There were also an increasing number of single-parent households and families with two working parents, and busy people couldn't – or wouldn't – find time to shop for food and cook meals at home. Finally, for many people, cooking is a chore that generates stress. A study by a Harvard University professor in 2017 found that only 10 per cent of Americans liked to cook – and this was down one-third from the same survey conducted fifteen years before.[8]

As a result of societal changes, deskilling and lack of interest in cooking, many more consumers now buy heat-and-eat prepared foods – canned soups, frozen dinners, microwaveable entrées and the like. Others just eat out more often. This has further diminished the need and the desire for traditional cookery skills. Lifestyle changes also encourage consumers to eat out more often. Many order too much at restaurants and fast-food outlets and then toss out what was uneaten.

Yet another cause of increased consumer waste is, ironically, national and global publicity about food safety. Rather than taking a perceived risk on food that looks, smells or tastes questionable, it is considered safer to just toss it out. Food is cheap, and there is plenty more at the shops. There is no need to take a chance on getting sick.

Down the Drain

In-sink garbage disposals, also called food-waste disposers, became commonplace in many homes and food-service operations by the 1960s. Today, about half of U.S. homes have in-sink garbage disposal units, but they are much less popular elsewhere in the world. Attached to the kitchen sink drain, the disposal shreds food waste into small granules that are washed down the drain, and from there into the sewer system, where sewage-treatment plants filter out the solid waste, which is sent to landfills.

Concerns about ground-up food waste have been raised for decades. Cooking grease that is washed down the drain can congeal, obstructing pipes and sewers. Such blockages cause overflows that are expensive to clear. Some municipalities have resisted the use of in-sink garbage disposal units in homes, and three countries – Portugal, Austria and the Netherlands – have banned their use. Environmentalists point out that composting food waste at home is a much greener option, and inexpensive indoor home composters can convert food waste into solid compost in less than a day with minimal use of electricity. The compost can be used in a home garden or collected and then distributed to fertilize plants in parks, garden allotments and nearby farms.

Water-treatment plants can use the sludge to produce methane on-site and convert it into biogas. Converting sewage sludge into methane is cheaper and more environmentally sound than sending food scraps to a landfill. However, wastewater containing ground-up food needs to be pumped to treatment plants, and this is an expensive, energy-intensive process. Proponents of garbage disposals argue that the pumping would be necessary anyway, as human waste as well as water from sinks, showers and baths still needs to be pumped. And they point to other advantages: food waste can be quickly and easily disposed of in the home so it doesn't start to smell or attract vermin. Garbage disposal units reduce the amount of food waste going to landfills (and save the cost of hauling it to the dump). Dissolved solids, including ground-up food waste, end up in wastewater treatment plants, which typically employ enzymes to convert the waste into carbon dioxide which, from an environmental standpoint, is better than the methane that would be produced if the food scraps ended up in landfill. Some wastewater and sewage-treatment facilities use anaerobic digestion technology to convert organic waste into biogas.

Several government projects have incorporated waste disposals into environmentally sustainable communities. In Malmö, Sweden, for instance, apartment buildings with disposals are hooked up to a separate system for turning food scraps into methane. Similar systems have been proposed in other cities.

Retailer Ploys

Historically, consumers shopped with awareness of what supplies were on hand in their home kitchen, planning to buy only what they needed to replace or complement it. List in hand, they restocked staples and bought needed ingredients, typically sticking to what was on the list. Supermarket executives realized they had to distract customers from ironclad adherence to their shopping lists and seduce them into making impulse purchases. In-store techniques for increasing sales included strategic placement of products (for example, stocking sweets on low shelves where children could reach them) and hard-to-resist sales and special offers that encouraged shoppers to buy more than they needed. Chains cut prices 'extra low' for the biggest 'family-size' packages and offered 'buy one get one free' (BOGOF) sales. Today, people shop less systematically and more impulsively, with the result that they often bring home more food than they can use. A recent study in the U.S. demonstrated that 14 per cent of home food waste was still in its original packaging with unexpired date labels.[9]

Anti-food-waste advocates have specifically opposed BOGOF offers, and some supermarket chains have eliminated them. France proposed a ban on supermarket discounts greater than 34 per cent on food, which would effectively eliminate BOGOF offers. In San Francisco, Farmstead, an on-demand grocery service start-up, has put a new, positive spin on the BOGOF concept and gained considerable goodwill for doing so. Farmstead has 'Buy One, Give One' specials on selected fruit and vegetables; for each item the customer buys, Farmstead donates the same item to a needy student.

For those who wish to avoid the entire experience of shopping for food, the advent of home-delivery meal kits has been a boon. Some services provide tailor-made ready-to-eat meals; others provide pre-measured ingredients needed for a specific meal, along with the required recipes. The companies that offer these services claim that they help cut down on food waste, but since each ingredient is enclosed in its own packet, bag or box, environmentalists complain that these services increase packaging waste. In response, some meal-kit delivery companies have switched to packaging that is fully recyclable. One recent study has concluded that 'meal kits have lower average greenhouse gas emissions than grocery store meals' and they may also produce less waste than grocery shopping.[10]

Restaurateurs, like retailers, beguile their customers into buying more food than they need. Many consumers spend more on meals eaten outside the home than they do on groceries. Fast-food chains have over the years devised a foolproof way to pull in customers: in the 1970s they began to feature 'supersized' menu selections, offering customers extra-large portions. Chain restaurants also offer LTO (limited time only) menu selections to encourage customers to order special items before the promotional period ends. Consumers fall prey to these sales techniques and frequently buy more food than they can consume; the leftovers, of course, end up in the bin. Likewise, eating on-the-go creates huge levels of packaging waste, most of which is not recyclable as it is made from mixed materials or is contaminated with food residue.

Many consumers seem to be unaware that they are throwing away perfectly good food, whether it's a packaged product that is a few days past its 'best by' date or a slightly soft apple that could be made into a sauce. Public awareness campaigns have been launched to help educate consumers about the problem of food waste – and its potential solutions. Possible fixes include teaching consumers how to repurpose leftovers; the use of meal-planning apps and high-tech kitchen tools and appliances; encouraging wider use of 'doggy bags'; instructing people on composting organic material in the home; and instituting home food-waste collection programmes.

Leftover and Waste-free Cookbooks

Traditionally, home cooks passed on to the next generation their knowledge of economical housekeeping – how to avoid wasting food and how to use up leftovers. By the eighteenth century, many cookbooks included advice on dealing with scraps or 'fragments', and on making and serving 'réchauffés' or 'made-over dishes'. Beginning in the late nineteenth century, books and pamphlets were published focusing on 'leftovers'.

The act of eating leftovers was a patriotic duty during the First World War. During the Depression, it became a necessity. During the Second World War, eating leftovers became a political, economic and moral issue. When the war and rationing ended, food prices began to decline relative to income. Saving and eating leftovers became a lower priority. During the 1950s, tossing out leftovers became a mark of middle-class status in the United States. Cookbook authors had to urge readers not to think of leftovers as dreary. One joke ran, 'The best way to serve leftovers is to somebody else.' When the cost of food began to rise during the early 1970s, leftovers re-emerged as a money saver. Cookbooks focusing on leftovers were published in many affluent countries, but when food prices subsequently declined, they fell from favour.

When the war on food waste got underway in 2009, another wave of 'use-it-up' cookbooks hit the culinary world. In the UK, Caroline Marson published *Love Food Hate Waste: The Cookbook*. In Italy, Letizia Nucciotti published *Avanzi popolo: l'arte di riciclare tutto quello che avanza in cucina: storia, ricette e consigli* (Leftovers People: The Art of Recycling All the Leftovers from Cooking: Stories, Recipes and Tips). In the u.s., Lynette Rohrer Shirk and Lara Starr published *The Frugal Foodie Cookbook: Waste-not Recipes for the Wise Cook*. Two years later Selina Juul teamed up with Danish chefs to publish *Stop spild af mad: en kogebog med mere* (Stop Waste of Food: A Cookbook and More) in 2011. In addition to offering readers advice on how to use leftovers it also educated the readers about food-waste issues. British chef Hugh Fearnley-Whittingstall's *River Cottage Love Your Leftovers: Recipes for the Resourceful Cook* (2015) offered tips on storing food properly to avoid waste. Dana Gunders's *Waste-free Kitchen Handbook* (2015) offers suggestions for shopping, portioning and using preservation methods to decrease waste.

Meal-planning Apps

A major cause of food waste at home is buying excessive amounts of perishables – fruit, vegetables, and meat and dairy products – that spoil before they can be eaten. This results from poor meal planning, neglecting to check the pantry before shopping, or succumbing to discount offers at the supermarket.

The introduction of meal-planning and recipe apps for smartphones may help shoppers resist the temptations posed by advertising and promotional gimmicks and instead buy only what they really need. Some apps, such as Cloud-Freezer, allow users to create an inventory of food items they already have at home; others, such as Pepperplate and

MealBoard, create shopping lists, enable meal planning and offer recipes. Catering to vegans, One Green Planet's Food Monster app helps reduce food waste at home by offering recipes like a 'mineral-packed, plant-based healing broth from your leftover vegetable scraps'.[11]

Online meal planners are also available, enabling subscribers to list the foods and ingredients they have on hand; this prompts the program to access recipes and generate shopping lists for items needed at the store. Online meal planners include Cook Smarts, Plan To Eat and Tesco's Real Food. Users can enter ingredients and the app offers a selection of recipes.

Yet another approach to decreasing consumer food waste is the UK-based app OLIO, that connects consumers with each other and local shops. It was launched in the UK at the end of 2015. Within four years the app had 1.6 million subscribers in 48 countries. They have shared more than 2.7 million portions of food between them. It has also raised an estimated $8.2 million in capital, proving that such projects can also make business sense. OLIO proclaims that it is 'The Food Sharing Revolution'.

Smart Refrigerators and Community Refrigerators

The advent of refrigerators and freezers in the twentieth century extended the shelf-life of many foods in supermarkets, food-service operations and homes. Produce could be preserved longer, meats could be frozen and leftovers could be safely put away for another day's meal. Refrigerators, freezers and kitchens got bigger as the century progressed, reflecting growing affluence and the abundance of food of all kinds. Ironically, overstocked homes contributed to waste as foods got pushed to the back of crowded fridges until they soured, spoiled or rotted and ended up in the rubbish bin.

New 'smart' refrigerators can help reduce that waste. They are equipped with built-in cameras and touchscreen technology with access to the Internet. The cameras provide wide-angle views of the inside of the refrigerator that the user can view on a smartphone. Touchscreens on the refrigerator door can perform online recipe searches, place shopping orders, post reminders and create lists in order to make shopping and meal planning more streamlined and efficient. Most operate on voice command, so that the user can verbally ask for information while cooking rather than touching the screen with wet or greasy fingers.

Other high-tech refrigerators have barcode detectors that track food stored in them, or RFID readers that detect and identify food products bearing RFID tags. These devices can tell the user what's in the refrigerator and also detect and report expiration dates on products that have freshness dates. Mainly used for commercial operations, these tracking devices allow for continuous monitoring of food stocks.

One creative solution to consumer food waste has been the advent of community refrigerators, also called 'solidarity fridges', and 'people's fridges'. The concept originated in Germany, when the online collective Foodsharing.de installed public refrigerators and storage shelves where anyone could drop off – or pick up – food items. They worked closely with German and European health officials to make sure no laws were violated. Today, Foodsharing.de has more than 7,500 outlets that promote the exchange of food and the reduction of waste.

The community refrigerator concept quickly spread to other countries. They usually operate under safety guidelines, such as no raw fish, meat or eggs, and no packaged goods past their use-by date. For those that accept home-cooked food, it must be marked with a date. The Community Fridge Network was formed in the UK to help coordinate and encourage community fridge operation. As of March 2019, fifty community fridges in the UK had redistributed an average of 25 tonnes of food each month.

Community fridge programmes do sometimes come up against public health regulations. Two graduate students in Davis, California, placed a glass-fronted refrigerator in their front garden with a sign reading, 'Take what you need. Leave what you don't.' Health officials shut them down for illegal food distribution.

Food Waste Collection

Many cities around the world now look at food waste as a resource and require collection of this waste from businesses and homes. Munich, Germany, was the first large European city to begin a collection programme. In 1983 the city introduced the 'Biotonne' (Organic Bin) – a covered plastic container – to receive kitchen and garden waste, which is then picked up by the city and converted into compost. Austria required the separate collection of organic waste beginning in 1995.

South Korea started requiring the separation of food from other waste in 1997 and implemented a 'pay-as-you-throw' programme in Seoul beginning in 2005. Its implementation was coupled with a major public relations campaign to gain support from consumers. Seven years later it was fully implemented in 4 million households. This system requires consumers to pay by weight for the food they throw away. The goal was to reduce food waste by creating a financial incentive to generate less garbage. The collected food waste is processed into animal feed or compost, or used to generate electricity. By 2015 household food waste had been reduced by 30 per cent, and by 2019 South Korea recycled 95 per cent of its food waste.[12] In the UK, the island of Guernsey implemented such a programme, and now many other communities are considering 'pay-as-you-throw' systems.

Bristol was the first city in the United Kingdom to roll out kerbside collection of food waste. The city council provided a kitchen container for food scraps and a large brown bin for pickup at the kerb on collection day. Other communities in England, Wales and Scotland have since developed kerbside food-waste collection systems. Barcelona began requiring residents to separate grass clipping, leaves and other organic waste along with food waste, to be collected for composting. Milan's programme began in November 2012 and became fully operational in 2014. Other cities that have introduced similar plans include Brussels, Dublin, Oslo and Växjö, Sweden. The European countries that are leaders in composting organic waste are Germany and France.

The San Francisco Board of Supervisors instituted kerbside collection of food waste in 2009. Its Mandatory

Recycling & Composting Ordinance required everyone to separate organic matter into compost bins. The resulting compost is sold for about $9 per cubic yard (0.77 m³). By 2013 more than 150 communities around the u.s. were picking up organic produce at the kerbside. Several states, such as Connecticut, Massachusetts, Rhode Island and Vermont, have banned the burial of organics in landfills, and other states and cities have pending legislation to do the same. The residents of New York City throw out about 14 million tonnes of food waste every year, and it costs the city about $400 million to pick it up and transport it to dumps as far away as South Carolina. In 2013 the city launched a voluntary programme for collecting organic waste from buildings with fewer than ten apartments. Within four years, New York City's voluntary organics-collection programme, which converts organic waste into compost and natural gas, was the largest in the United States, and it is scheduled to expand rapidly during the next few years.

Food-waste collection is not without its challenges. If the receptacles don't close tightly, unpleasant odours can seep out and the bins can provide a place for insects and rodents to feast. These problems increase if collections are missed or delayed. Also, if consumers are not thoroughly informed about what to put into the containers (nothing except organic material), they may mix in other kinds of waste, which creates difficulties for composting and biogas production.

Educating for Saving Food

Programmes have been undertaken throughout the world to help educate consumers about food waste. They have focused on pre-collegiate education, colleges and universities and consumer education programmes.

Pre-collegiate schools around the world have adopted programmes to educate students about food waste and offer potential solutions. The World Wildlife Fund launched the Food Waste Warrior programme targeting primary and secondary schools in the U.S. It encourages students to audit their school's food waste and learn how food impacts the environment. Pre-collegiate schools have launched 'share tables' where students can place unopened food and drinks, allowing other students to take additional helpings of food or beverages at no cost to them. This educates all students about the need to reduce food waste while also catering for those students in need.

Universities have also developed programmes to cut down on waste in their own institutions and teach students about the importance of reducing waste. Student-led programmes have also targeted food waste in their universities and communities. One student-led effort, the Food Recovery Network, was launched to fight food waste and hunger at the University of Maryland, and by 2019 had expanded to 230 chapters in 44 states.

The James Beard Foundation established 'Creating a Full-use Kitchen', an online waste-minimization course for culinary instructors and students. The Foundation also published the *Waste Not* cookbook, coupled with 'Waste

Not Wednesdays', where those who observe the day try to eliminate food waste.

Other programmes have focused on educating consumers. In the UK, Tesco partnered with Jamie Oliver to start a cookery school to teach hundreds of community cooks how best to use surplus food and how to stop food from going to waste. Studies of the most effective methods of teaching food-waste reduction suggest various approaches: for instance, stressing the practical benefits (you save money on your food bill) or inducing guilt (how can you waste food when there are an estimated 795 million people around the world starving, malnourished or living in food-insecure households?). Another potential solution is to encourage consumers to record what food they toss out. A German survey found that asking consumers to record their patterns of purchasing and throwing away food led to a significant reduction in waste.

When research demonstrated that millennials (aged eighteen to 34) in the UK were the age group that threw away the most food, the UK's Waste and Resources Action Programme (WRAP) launched a multichannel campaign using Facebook, YouTube, Twitter and Instagram to focus on millennials living in urban areas. Despite massive public education campaigns in the UK, a major study found that household food waste had increased by 4.4 per cent since 2012.[13] There are several reasons for this. One survey found that 24.1 per cent of respondents said that they just did not have the time to worry about food waste. Others believed that they were already making considerable efforts. More than three-quarters of respondents claimed that they wasted less food than did the average person, while only 13.6 per cent felt they were wasting more.[14]

In New Zealand, Love Food Hate Waste launched a consumer education programme in 2015. An audit study of bins during the following three years concluded that New Zealanders who were aware of the campaign reduced their food waste by more than 27 per cent. However, the study found that on average in 2017/18 households were still throwing away 3.15 kilograms (6.9 lb) of food per week compared with 3.17 kilograms (6.98 lb) in 2014/15.[15]

Studies that have examined the effects of awareness campaigns are relatively few and report mixed results. Sligo County Council in Ireland launched a community education programme to improve the capture of food waste in 2014. Programmes included door-to-door education and distribution of compostable bags to households. The research project examining the programme concluded that relatively low-cost consumer education could have a significant effect on preventing food waste.[16] Other studies have indicated that education programmes have resulted in modest but statistically insignificant reductions in food waste. Education programmes are important to alert consumers to issues of food waste, but they do not necessarily convert attitudes into behavioural change.

In addition to food waste, consumers and consumer-facing businesses throw out massive amounts of containers and packaging, such as bottles, cans, plastic wrappings, cardboard boxes and wax-treated paper containers. People litter streets, motorways and parks with plastic boxes, paper bags and foam cups from fast food and takeaway establishments, exacerbating the problem of food waste. Food- and beverage-related waste are the topics of the next chapter.

7
FOOD-RELATED WASTE

Until the early twentieth century, grains, flours, beans, coffee, tea and dried fruit were typically shipped in wooden boxes, barrels or sacks. Customers or clerks reached into the container and measured out the desired amount into a paper packet or cloth bag. This worked well enough, but the open containers exposed the food to dust, dirt, mould, moisture and infestation by vermin.

The food-packaging revolution began in the second half of the nineteenth century with the inventions of tin canning and resealable glass jars. Flat-bottomed paper bags, introduced in the mid-nineteenth century, could be filled with bulk groceries scooped from a box or barrel. Paper bags and paperboard boxes were transformed by the invention of the offset press in 1879, permitting brands, logos and other identifying marks to be printed on bags and boxes, and on the labels for bottles and cans. With the cheap and rapid production of food packaging, the retail scene changed. Packaging could bear distinctive colours, lettering and eye-catching artwork that set branded goods apart from generics. New trademarked food products came on the market, and grocery stores widened the range of items that they stocked.

Food-related packaging includes everything from the large timber pallets and drums used to transport bulk food products, to the paper, cardboard, plastic, glass and metal used in the boxes, bags, bottles and cans that line super-market shelves, to the single-use dishes and containers that serve meals at food-service operations. Packaging is indis-pensable: it protects food products from physical damage and preserves their flavour and nutritional value. It enables food products to travel safely over long distances from farms and processing operations to retailers, and allows consumers to store food for weeks, months and even years.

Most food-related packaging cannot be recycled and so the majority of it ends up in landfills. A study published in 2007 estimated that approximately 20 per cent of municipal solid waste in the u.s. consisted of food-packaging materials, which accounted for almost two-thirds of total packaging waste by volume.[1] Packaging also contributes to pollution of the water supply and the oceans. Some packaging materials, especially plastics, can survive for tens of thousands of years in landfills without decomposing completely.

Plastic Packaging and Containers

The twentieth century brought another food-packaging revolution when petrochemical companies began to turn petroleum into plastic. By the 1940s plastic was the miracle packaging solution for food and beverages: it was cheap, lightweight and extremely versatile. It has since evolved into thousands of different products. Plastic is virtually indestructible, waterproof and flexible. Hard plastics are used in making jugs, bottles, cutlery, dishes and microwave-able containers; soft plastics are used for cling film, shrink wrap, sandwich bags, produce bags and shopping bags. Clear plastic lets customers see what they are buying, and the sight of tempting food encourages impulse purchases.

Plastic protects food from light, air and moisture to maintain its wholesomeness and nutritional qualities, and it is impervious to most bacteria. Plastic can keep perishable foods fresh: for instance, a thin plastic shrink-wrap film, such as polyolefin, can extend the shelf life of a cucumber up to two weeks. The uses of plastic in food packaging have grown over the past few decades because it offers many func-tional advantages over traditional materials such as glass and metal: thermosealability, microwaveability, optical properties (it makes the food look good) and the potential to be formed into myriad sizes and shapes. It replaces durable dishes and cutlery that require washing, freeing restaurateurs to toss used straws, plates, cups, forks and spoons in the bin.

More plastic was manufactured during the first decade of the twenty-first century than had been produced during the entire twentieth century; in 2014 some 300 million metric tons of plastic were produced globally. Of that, only about 10 per cent was recycled and 79 per cent ended up in landfill. It is projected that the amount of plastic produced annually will triple by 2050.[2]

Plastic bottles, bags, wrappers, straws and polystyrene takeaway containers and coffee cups make up an estimated 85 per cent of the food-packaging waste stream. These 'indispensable' everyday items have serious drawbacks: they are not biodegradable and even the types that can be recycled still end up in landfill. Plastic can survive for hundreds of thousands of years without decomposing, and discarded plastics accumulate in landfill, harm wildlife, pollute the environment, blight coastlines and infest the oceans.

Styrofoam and Polystyrene Foam

Of particular concern to environmentalists has been Styrofoam, the trademarked brand for varieties of expanded polystyrene foam, a thermoplastic product that is light-weight, durable and moisture-resistant. It was devised in 1941 by researchers at the Dow Chemical Company. By the 1960s it had been widely adopted by food-service operations for coffee cups, hamburger boxes (the one-piece 'clamshell' serves as both plate and lid) and cold drinks, as well as egg cartons, disposable plates and trays, and protective sleeves for glass soda bottles.

Styrofoam and related polystyrene products such as kay-lite (EPS) have serious environmental drawbacks: for starters, the manufacturing process releases 57 chemical by-products that pollute the environment, as well as producing liquid and solid waste that require special disposal. It cannot be economically recycled. It does break down into small particles, but they can take an estimated five hundred years to degrade completely; if incinerated, Styrofoam produces toxic emissions.

Styrene, the precursor to polystyrene, breaks down when heated and readily migrates from packaging into food and beverages. Drink a hot beverage from a foam cup, for instance, and you're ingesting small particles of polystyrene.

The migration of styrene into human fat cells was first detected in 1972 and subsequent research has supplied further confirmation. Until recently the health effects of styrene on the human body remained unclear, although many health experts were concerned and it seemed likely that styrene was a possible human carcinogen. In 2014 the National Research Council of the National Institute of Health in the United States officially proclaimed that styrene was 'reasonably anticipated to be a human carcinogen'.[3]

In recent years a number of local governments have taken action to eliminate Styrofoam and polystyrene foam from their waste stream. The City Council of Berkeley, California, banned all single-use polystyrene foam products, including plates, cups and clamshell boxes, and it imposed a 25-cent tax on all disposable cups. San Francisco made it illegal for restaurants and food vendors to use Styrofoam food service ware and required the use of recyclable or compostable food ware. The state of Maine passed a law in April 2019 prohibiting convenience stores, restaurants, grocery stores, farm stands and coffee shops from using containers made of polystyrene, which will go into effect in 2021.

Many other cities around the world have also instituted bans. Muntinlupa (Philippines), Oxford (England), Toronto, Paris and other local governments have banned single-use polystyrene foam and other non-recyclable plastic containers for food service and other uses. Fifteen cities and states in Mexico have passed laws intended to reduce the use of disposable plastics. Other municipalities have committed to eliminating single-use plastic containers and cutlery in future years. Several countries have banned polystyrene containers.

Restaurant trade groups and manufacturers of the containers have opposed these prohibitions and challenged them in court, and in some cases the bans have been overturned.

Some fast-food chains have phased out Styrofoam cups. After considerable pressure, McDonald's switched from Styrofoam clamshells to paper boxes in August 1990. However, the chain continued to use polystyrene foam coffee cups until 2013, when they were replaced with double-walled waxed-paper hot cups. KFC replaced Styrofoam buckets with reusable polypropylene tubs. The lids are marked 'KFC Reusable, Microwave & Top Rack Dishwasher Safe' to encourage customers to keep them for reuse. The new tubs require 25 per cent less energy to produce and generate 50 per cent less greenhouse gases than do other containers, according to The Greener Package (GP), an organization devoted to sustainable packaging. A study indicated that customers did save and reuse the containers, and GP gave KFC an award for significantly reducing the environmental footprint of its packaging.

PET Bottles and Cutlery

The polyethylene terephthalate (PET) bottle was invented in 1973 by Nathan Wyeth at DuPont, the American chemical company. He developed a system of moulding plastic that enabled DuPont to produce lightweight, clear, resilient bottles. Within a few years, PET bottles had become the standard for the beverage industry.

Plastic bottles cannot be refilled for resale, so the beverage industry and manufacturers of plastic packaging have supported recycling initiatives that require local governments to collect, sort and process plastic waste – a complex, time-consuming, costly task. Some localities charge a 'deposit' fee on soda bottles and cans; if the container is returned, the deposit is refunded and the container is recycled. (Of course, consumers can also recycle cans and bottles themselves, forgoing the deposit.) In 2006 Americans alone discarded an estimated 50 billion plastic bottles, which contribute to an estimated 1.5 billion kilograms (3.2 billion lb) of total unrecycled plastic garbage.[4]

Plastic-bottle recycling statistics vary from country to country, but in the United States only about 31 per cent of PET bottles are recycled. PET Container Recycling Europe, a Brussels-based non-profit organization representing PET manufacturers, reported that in 2014 more than 57 per cent of all bottles sold in Europe were recycled.[5] In Switzerland, an estimated 93 per cent of beverage packaging was recycled by 2012.[6]

In addition to plastic bottles, restaurants and food-service operations use massive amounts of plastic cutlery. Globally, an estimated 350 billion plastic forks, knives and spoons are discarded every year. Few are recycled. France banned plastic cutlery in 2016. Alternatives to throwaway and non-biodegradable plastic cutlery have emerged, including compostable and/or reusable utensils made of wood, bamboo and other plant materials. If they end up in the bin, at least they will degrade. Bakeys Foods in Hyderabad, India, has taken this a step further with a line of edible cutlery that looks like wood and comes in three flavours – plain, sweet and savoury – to complement the meal.

Plastic Bags

Although most plastic bags are used only once, they are made of sturdy stuff that can take hundreds of years to decompose. Most plastic bags, like other potentially recyclable plastic objects, end up in landfills. According to the Natural Resources Defense Council, the average u.s. family carries home 1,500 plastic bags from shops each year. The *Wall Street Journal* estimates that 100 billion plastic bags are thrown away each year in the United States alone. Manufacturing these bags consumes 12 million barrels of oil per year.[7] Some supermarket chains collect used bags for recycling, but very few customers take advantage of this option – it's a low priority and just too inconvenient. Plastic bags make up only about 0.3 per cent of the total waste in municipal waste dumps,[8] but discarded bags can end up clogging sewer systems and have injured or killed birds, animals and fish that consume them or become entangled in them.

A more dramatic solution to phasing out single-use bags is to tax them or to ban them outright. Bangladesh became the first country to ban thin plastic bags in 2002. In the same year, Ireland instituted a highly effective tax on plastic bags (called the 'plastax') that reduced plastic bag litter by an estimated 95 per cent.[9] Other countries, including Haiti, South Africa, Rwanda, China, Italy and Mexico, followed suit. Kenya has outlawed the production, sale and use of plastic bags; violators risk imprisonment for up to four years and a $40,000 fine.

France has legislated against the use of plastic bags, proposing to replace them with compostable bags made of a combination of plastic and potato starch or corn starch. Some of Australia's states and territories – Tasmania, South Australia, the Northern Territory and the Australian Capital Territory – have banned the use of thin plastic bags. Supermarket chains, such as Woolworths, Big W, bws, Dan Murphy's and Cellarmasters, have stopped offering plastic bags to customers throughout Australia. Cities and counties in the u.s. have instituted bans and taxes. California passed a state-wide tax on plastic bags in 2014 and five years later New York state passed a similar law.

In the uk, Wales began taxing single-use plastic bags in 2011; Northern Ireland did so in 2013; Scotland in 2014; and England in 2016. Theresa May, the British prime minister from July 2016 to July 2019, called plastic waste 'one of the great environmental scourges of our time'. She planned to extend the 5p levy on plastic bags, asked supermarkets to introduce 'plastic-free aisles' and argued for the elimination of 'avoidable' plastic waste within a quarter of a century. To achieve this objective, taxes may be levied to discourage production of some items, such as unrecyclable takeaway containers. The opposition argued that plastic-free aisles were 'too simplistic' and that eliminating plastic food packaging might increase food waste, because the packaging protects and extends the shelf life of food products.

Straw Wars

During the 1960s, many restaurants around the world began to replace paper straws with single-use plastic straws made of polypropylene, a petroleum product. They were cheap, easy to make, easy to store and easy to use. An estimated 500 million straws are used each day in the U.S. alone, which adds up to 175 billion straws per year. Single-use plastic straws have been identified as the 'world's most wasteful commodity'.

Plastic straws are used by consumers for a matter of minutes. They can be recycled, but the vast majority are not. They are among the most common items found on beaches and waterways and are among the top ten items found in marine plastic debris. Like other oceanic plastic, they harm sea life, and when they break down into microplastics they can enter the food chain and eventually end up in our bodies.

Several initiatives, such as 'Strawless in Seattle', 'The Last Plastic Straw', 'No to Plastic Straws', 'Straws Suck' and the 'Be Straw Free' campaign, have been launched to end the use of single-use plastic straws. Restaurant chains in some countries, such as South Africa, Costa Rica and Thailand, have implemented bans on plastic straws. José Andrés, the Washington, DC-based restaurateur, has his staff give out plastic straws only upon request, and only 5 per cent of customers do ask for them. Andrés asks: 'Can humanity survive without plastic straws? I think so.'[10] In January 2018 a bill was introduced into the California legislature to make it illegal for restaurant servers to give customers plastic straws unless requested. The Walt Disney Company is in the midst of eliminating single-use plastic straws and plastic stirrers at its parks and McDonald's announced that it is shifting from plastic to paper straws at its UK locations.

Irish Pubs Global, a trade association of 8,500 pubs around the world, asked its members to stop providing customers with non-recyclable plastic straws. Forty pubs pledged to phase out plastic straws by the end of the year. Glasgow City Council outlawed the use of plastic straws in its building in January 2018; the Scottish Parliament soon followed by outlawing the use of plastic straws in the parliament building, and there were plans to outlaw plastic straws entirely in Scotland in the future; and England will ban plastic straws (and plastic stirrers) in 2020. Canada plans to ban single-use plastics by 2021.

The European Parliament banned a wide range of single-use plastic items, including straws, cotton buds and cutlery by 2021. Several major UK food service and hospitality companies have pledged to eliminate plastic straws, but journalists investigating those businesses found little evidence of follow-through and questioned whether the 'straw pledges' were 'bending the truth'.[11]

Some restaurants and other retail food operations have gone back to using paper straws that can be recycled with other paper waste. Others now use straws made from biodegradable plastic, paper and other products, but these are 20 to 30 per cent more expensive that the plastic straws currently in use. Some restaurants have replaced plastic straws with reusable ones made of metal, glass or bamboo, but these are not cost effective for use in fast food or takeaway operations. Some eating and drinking establishments give customers plastic straws only on request, and many state this policy on their menus. Still others hand out Twizzlers – hollow 'liquorice' twists about the size of a straw that come in various flavours and can be used to slurp up some beverages. Starbucks has announced that they plan to phase out plastic straws by 2020.

Companies manufacture biodegradable straws that reportedly have the look and the feel of a regular plastic straw. One company, Loliware in New York, makes Lolistraws that are also edible. They are made from seaweed, organic sweeteners and flavours and colours derived from lemons, limes, strawberries, cinnamon, green apples and ginger. They are both edible and compostable straws that have a shelf life of two years.

The Paper Cup Manifesto

In the United States alone, an estimated 60 billion single-use coffee cups end up in landfills every year. Some fast-food chains and coffee shops have switched from plastic and Styrofoam to cups made of recyclable cardboard lined with a thin layer of polyethylene. The plastic lining inside these cups keeps the beverage hot and prevents the cardboard from becoming soggy. Users believe these cups to be recyclable – and they are – but some must be processed at specialized facilities: they cannot be recycled with other paper and card-board. Other biodegradable cups are made from plant-based plastic – called a bioplastic – that is fully biodegradable and thus disposable either in a paper-recycling or food waste bin.

During the past two decades the UK has experienced a rapid growth in chain coffee shops, and almost half of all their hot drinks are served in polyethylene-lined disposable cups. Some coffee shops have separate disposal bins for these cups so they can be sent to special recycling facilities. Most cups, however, end up in on-street recycling bins, which creates a costly waste contamination problem for recyclers. Cups also litter streets, roadsides and beaches. As a result, less than one-quarter of the 2.5 billion single-use cups thrown away in Great Britain each year are recycled. High-profile chef and anti-waste campaigner Hugh Fearnley-Whittingstall targeted these single-use cups in an episode of his series *Hugh's War on Waste*, which aired on the BBC in 2016. Several large chains in the UK, including Costa Coffee, Starbucks, McDonald's, KFC and Pret A Manger, signed a 'Paper Cup Manifesto', a voluntary pledge to improve customer knowledge about the recyclability of these cups and to improve cup-recycling rates by 2020.

The coffee chains in the UK seemed to have made some progress in this effort, but according to the House of Commons' Environmental Audit Committee, most companies have failed to take action that would effectively tackle the problem. The committee called for a tax of 25p (34 cent), or 'latte levy', on each single-use cup, and for improved labelling to avoid customer confusion about recyclability. To encourage companies to transition to reusable or completely recyclable coffee cups, the committee called for a ban on single-use cups by 2023.[12] Some chains already offer customers a discount if they bring in their own (reusable) coffee mugs; Pret A Manger, for instance, takes 50p (68 cents) off the price of the beverage.

Other national and local governments are considering measures against single-use coffee cups. The Irish Green Party wants an outright ban on non-recyclable beverage containers. In the German city of Freiburg, the reusable plastic 'Freiburg Cup' is keeping disposable cups out of the waste stream. City governments provide the cups to coffee shops, and customers pay a refundable deposit fee per cup when buying coffee. The cafés are responsible for sanitizing the cups, which last for about four hundred uses. Similar experiments have been undertaken in other places in Germany.

Litter and Pollution

Many food-related paper products, coffee cups, single-use containers, bottles and wrappers never make it into rubbish bins, let alone recycling bins. In throwaway cultures, foodrelated packaging makes up the bulk of the litter that ends up on streets, gardens, pavements and beaches, along motorways and in waterways and oceans. Such litter pollutes the soil and water, mars the landscape, blights coastlines and endangers wildlife. Even when this waste, such as food-soiled paper wrappers, is placed in bins, it is not recyclable and much of it ends up in landfills or incinerators.

A considerable volume of litter comes from the tons of paper, plastic and foam products used by fast-food chains, takeaway restaurants, gas station kiosks, newsagents, supermarkets and other retail operations that offer food and beverages to take out. It costs less to buy disposable serving ware than it does to wash durable dishes and cutlery, and breakage is a non-issue. These establishments place waste bins where they are most visible and convenient, and post signs encouraging customers to 'put trash in its place'. But people on the move may not care about littering – especially when away from their own neighbourhood. It's just easier to throw litter out of the window or leave it on a roadside picnic table. Retail food chains sponsor community activities, such as motorway trash clean-ups, to counteract the bad press connected with litter. But the problem of discarded food packaging persists throughout the world.

As much as 70 per cent of the sales in many fast food and takeaway outlets consists of orders not eaten on the premises. When customers eat in their cars or elsewhere, even more litter ends up on streets and roadsides. Fed up with cleaning streets and public spaces strewn with burger wrappers, chip boxes, soda cans, cups, spoons, napkins, crisp packets and gum wrappers, cities and communities around the world began to tax the types of packaging most likely to end up as litter in public places. Ireland passed an anti-litter law in 2003 that taxed chewing gum, polystyrene food wrappers and plastic containers. A 2006 study in Oakland, California, concluded that 20 per cent of the city's litter came from food retailers, so the city council imposed a tax on these businesses, based on their gross sales, to cover litter removal. (Businesses that supported local rubbish clean-ups were charged less, or exempted entirely.) The following year, Chicago began taxing 'to go' fast-food orders. While litter laws have not stopped or reduced the volume of such waste, the taxes have mitigated the cost of cleaning it up.

Plastic litter isn't a problem only in developed countries. In Yaoundé, Cameroon, plastic bottles and containers block drains and exacerbate flooding during the rainy seasons in the flood-prone capital. Coeur d'Afrique (Heart of Africa), a non-profit that aids the underprivileged, pays unemployed youth in Cameroon to collect and sort the plastic, which is then converted into slabs that can be used in construction projects. A similar programme was launched in Tanzania; by February 2017, nearly 1 million kilograms of waste had been turned into 'plastic lumber' that can be used for fences, beams and signposts.[13]

Despite these programmes, far too much plastic litter still ends up in rivers, lakes and oceans throughout the world. Today, plastic (including food and beverage containers, plastic fishnets, microbeads from straws and bags, and so on) accounts for 80 per cent of global marine litter. About one-third of the fish caught off the coast of England are believed to contain particles of plastic.[14] A 2014 study estimated that there were 'at least 5.25 trillion plastic particles weighing 268,940 tons' floating at sea.[15] So much plastic has been found in the Pacific Ocean that parts of it have been designated 'The Great Pacific Garbage Patch'. In marine ecosystems, waste plastic has a harmful impact on aquatic organisms and consuming plastic particles can disturb reproductive functions. The National Oceanic and Atmospheric Administration in the U.S. concluded that roughly two hundred different marine species worldwide had been harmed – injured, sickened or killed – by plastic debris.

Plastic is also a potential threat to human health. In freshwater systems and oceans, plastic can break down into nanoscopic particles called microplastics, which are ingested by plankton and fish that mistake the plastic for food. The plastic then travels up the marine food chain, eventually ending up in fish and seafood consumed by humans. Plastic fibres also contaminate tap water. Microplastics can be carriers of harmful chemicals and potential human pathogens, but their short- and long-term effects on human health have not yet been determined.

A study published in 2015 found that more than a quarter of the fish and more than half of the shellfish sold in markets in Indonesia and California contained plastic particles and small synthetic fibres from clothes, diapers and cigarette butts. Microplastics were found in mussels from locations as far apart as the Arctic Ocean and the Chinese coast in a 2017 study.[16] Despite attempts to promote and legislate recycling, the amount of plastic waste is projected to surpass the total weight of fish in the sea by 2050.[17]

The United Nations launched the Clean Seas campaign to fight against marine plastic litter and save the oceans from irreversible damage. It works in cooperation with the Global Partnership of Marine Litter, a group of non-profit organizations, governments, international agencies and businesses, to reduce the production and consumption of non-recoverable and single-use plastic. More than sixty countries had signed on to the campaign by the end of 2019.

The impact that plastic has on the ocean, wildlife and public health was the focus of an episode of David Attenborough's documentary series *Blue Planet II*. The programme identified plastic and climate change as the biggest threats to the oceans. The documentary generated widespread concern about plastics, and it reportedly inspired Queen Elizabeth to ban single-use plastics, such as straws and bottles, from Buckingham Palace and other royal estates. Attenborough ended the show with the words, 'The future of all life now depends on us.'

The Courtauld Commitment

Packaging waste occurs throughout the food supply system, and historically most of it has ended up in garbage dumps. In u.s. landfill sites the amount of food packaging doubled between the years 1960 and 1996. Fast-food packaging and plastics used in food and beverage packaging demonstrated significant growth rates during this time. In all, food packaging accounted for about 12 per cent of the total volume of what was tossed into u.s. landfill, but additional amounts of food end up there due to the failure of packaging or the failure of consumers to repackage bulk food purchases properly.[18]

In the uk, the Waste and Resources Action Programme (wrap) was created in 2000. wrap's initial concern was reducing the amount of packaging and other materials that ended up in landfills.

wrap encouraged grocery retailers and food and drink manufacturers to sign onto a series of agreements called the Courtauld Commitment (2005), which were launched at the Courtauld Gallery in London. By doing so, they voluntarily agree to reduce food-related packaging by 5 per cent in manufacturing and retail, and to improve packaging design and recyclability in the grocery supply chain without increasing the carbon impact. More than fifty retailers and manufacturers signed on. The deadline for these commitments was 2015 and the signatories exceeded their commitments by reducing packing waste by more than 7 per cent, to less than 3 million tonnes – mostly due to increased recycling and shifts in the composition of packaging materials.[19] Between 2005 and 2009 the signatories reported that they decreased food waste by 670,000 tonnes and reduced packaging by 520,000 tonnes.

The Courtauld Commitment spurred research into more eco-friendly packaging. Waitrose, the British grocery store chain, developed a new box for its gluten-free (legume-based) pastas, using waste peas, beans and lentils that didn't meet quality standards for pasta production. The boxes are made with 15 per cent of this material. The package eliminates the need for an interior plastic sleeve, its production gives off 20 per cent less emissions and it is completely recyclable.[20]

Reducing Packaging

Food packers have spent decades trying to reduce waste by extending the shelf life of food products. Food packagers agree that food waste is a serious problem but argue that the way to reduce it may be more packaging, not less. The American Institute for Packaging and the Environment (AMERIPEN), a packaging solutions firm, argues that,

> The prevention of food waste not only saves food from going to waste, but also results in six times greater GHG [greenhouse gas] emissions savings than composting, seven times greater than anaerobic digestion and three times more than that of redistribution.[21]

With the renewed interest in decreasing waste, packaging manufacturers have reduced the amount of cardboard, plastic and other materials used in their products, and started to make packaging more recyclable. Manufacturers of grocery bags use untreated paper, which is highly biodegradable. It decomposes relatively quickly, as biological agents such as fungi and bacteria convert it into compost; it can also be recycled and made into other biodegradable products. Some non-biodegradable packages, such as glass bottles and metal cans, are highly recyclable, but they must be separated from other waste and transported to processing facilities, which consumes fossil fuels and other resources.

Reducing packaging saves money for food corporations, and around the world many have made commitments to do this. Marks & Spencer cut plastic use by redesigning and repackaging more than 140 products. Walmart unveiled a Sustainable Packaging Playbook describing the steps the company will take to achieve its 'zero waste to landfill' goal in Canada, Japan, the UK and the U.S. by 2025. Cranswick, PepsiCo and Unilever committed to making 100 per cent of their packaging recyclable, recoverable or compostable by 2025.

Those who oppose plastic packaging claim that it is designed to highlight branding rather than preserve food, and that it helps 'engrain a "single-use" culture in consumers' minds, encouraging users to thoughtlessly throw away vast amounts of packaging rather than considering more sustainable alternatives, such as using reusable containers or buying products in bulk'.[22] Standing their ground, plastic manufacturers maintain that reducing plastic will increase food waste. They project that without plastics, supermarket food waste would increase by one-third, and there would also be more waste generated during transportation and in the home. Instead of eliminating plastics, they prefer to encourage recycling and to work towards replacing non-biodegradable plastics with biodegradable ones where possible.

Many food producers are now 'light-weighting' their packaging. An example is the Greenshield box introduced by Pacific Seafood, one of the largest seafood companies in North America. The box is 100 per cent recyclable and uses fewer resources than other packaging, so there's less to recycle. Consumer-products giant Unilever committed to reducing the weight of its packaging by one-third by 2020. Beverage companies have reduced the amount of plastic and aluminium in their bottles and cans. 'Light-weighting' reduces costs, material consumption, transportation fuel and the amount of packaging trucked to landfills. Light-weighted containers, however, still contain plastic. Anti-plastic advocates have called for the end of all plastic containers and packaging – even for a total ban on all plastic products.

The global campaign against single-use plastic has produced results. The European Union declared war on plastic waste when it adopted a strategy to require all plastic packaging to be recyclable or reusable by 2030. Some large retailers provide alternatives to unrecyclable plastic containers. In February 2018, Ekoplaza, a Dutch supermarket chain, opened a plastic-free aisle, where all food is contained in metal, glass, cardboard or biodegradable plastic.

Some communities have been officially recognized as plastic-free. Penzance in Cornwall was certified as the UK's first 'Plastic Free Coastline Community' in December 2017. Aberporth in Wales was declared plastic-free in 2018. Additional communities in the UK and other countries are working to attain plastic-free designations. By March 2019

more than 170 countries pledged to significantly reduce
single-use plastic products by 2030.[23]

Biodegradable and Compostable Products

The fact that a considerable amount of food is thrown away
while still in its original packaging poses yet another serious
problem: before the food waste can be fed to animals,
composted, converted into biogas or upcycled into products,
the packaging has to be removed. This is a complicated and
costly process, so discarded packaged food is likely to end up
in a landfill or incinerator.

Bioplastic is a promising development that could go a long
way towards solving this problem. It can be made from corn,
potatoes, used cooking oil, rice, feathers, tapioca, palm fibre,
castor beans, soybeans, wheat fibre, sugar cane, shells, seaweed, algae, paper, wood and a wide variety of other organic
products. Bioplastic bottles were developed in the early years
of the twenty-first century. The Coca-Cola Company introduced completely recyclable PlantBottles made from sugar
cane and other plant materials. By 2015 about 30 per cent of
all Coca-Cola bottles in North America were PlantBottles,
although worldwide only 7 per cent of Coca-Cola's bottles
were made from plants. Critics have pointed out that
Coca-Cola's PlantBottles are non-biodegradable and that
'recyclable' does not mean that they are actually recycled.

In February 2011 the Canadian company redleaf water,
in collaboration with ENSO Plastics, introduced the 'Bio
Bottle', a biodegradable and recyclable PET bottle that does
not require special handling for recycling. According to

third-party reviews, Bio Bottles will disappear in landfills after one to fifteen years – a small fraction of the time required for other PET bottles to degrade. SodaStream International announced the release of its own Bio Bottle, which is used for the soda flavourings sold by the company (its main product is a do-it-yourself beverage carbonation system). Other companies use up to 50 per cent of recycled material in their bottles.

UK-based Iceland Foods announced plans to create new packaging from recyclable paper and pulp to replace plastic containers, which Iceland is scheduled to eliminate by 2023. During the last decade, McDonald's claims to have reduced waste by 30 per cent in its food preparation and supply systems. McDonald's outlets in New Zealand have entirely eliminated plastic: all packaging received by customers is made from recycled or other eco-friendly materials; it can be thrown out with organic waste and will decompose within ninety days. The company has announced that by 2025 all packaging received by customers at all of its 37,000 outlets will be recyclable.

Bioplastic is biodegradable, but not all bioplastic is compostable. Polylactic acid (PLA) is a compostable clear film that is made from plant products, such as corn-starch, and can be used to fabricate bags and wrappers. Starch-based biodegradable packaging products, including shopping bags, are already on the market, as are compostable bags made from the milk protein casein. Compostable plastic can also be made from polyhydroxyalkanoate (PHA), a naturally occurring polymer that biodegrades with reportedly no harmful effects to the environment.

It is made using unprocessed feedstocks rather than directly from oil. Another eco-friendly packaging innovation was developed by Evoware, an Indonesian company. Its seaweed-based packaging is used for burger wraps and coffee and dry seasoning bags. It is edible and compostable. It dissolves in warm water, has a shelf life of two years and is preservative-free. The Saltwater Brewery in Delray Beach, Florida, converts used barley and hops into biodegradable 'Eco Six Pack Rings', which are sold to other can manufacturers to help protect marine life from plastic.

PepsiCo went a different way for packaging its SunChips, a brand of multigrain chips (crisps) that the company wanted to position as eco-friendly. PepsiCo announced in 2009 that the packaging for SunChips was completely biodegradable, made from plant-based material that would break down within fourteen weeks of being in a compost pile. '100% Compostable Chip Package' was emblazoned on the bag. But the material made loud crackly noises when handled, and customers complained. PepsiCo introduced a quieter biodegradable bag design in 2011. How many customers actually compost the bag is unclear, but it seems like a step in the right direction.

Researchers continue to seek ways to make single-use coffee cups eco-friendlier. If the waterproof lining on the inside is plant-based, the cup can be composted along with other paper products. Manufacturers have produced coffee cups that are completely recyclable, and companies are evaluating them for possible use. For instance, Frugalpac in the UK manufactures a 'Frugal Cup' made of recycled paper. It can be processed in standard recycling facilities alongside other paper materials. Biodegradable plastic can be sent either to the plastic waste or paper waste recycling centres.

Unlike biodegradable materials, recyclable grades of plastic need to be downcycled. Many plastics described as biodegradable or compostable still need to be separated and collected separately from other plastic waste, and some must be sent to separate industrial composting facilities. This causes confusion for many consumers who throw biodegradable packaging into plastic-recycling containers or toss biodegradable plastic into food-waste containers.

Food producers have an array of compostable alternatives, made from plant fibres or starches, to choose from. Advanced cellulose films and paper, for instance, provide good barriers for oxygen, carbon dioxide and water vapour, and several cellulose fibre-based packaging products have been commercialized that provide an alternative to plastic. Not all compostable packaging works in every situation. Some types are adequate when distribution of a product is limited and local, but if the food company grows and products need to be transported greater distances, compostable packaging may no longer be durable enough for the job.

Packaging Innovations

The vacuum packaging process, created in the 1950s, removes air from the package prior to sealing. The first commercial application of vacuum packaging to perishable food was in the processing of whole turkeys. Vacuum packing reduced bacteria counts and gave meat, cheese and other perishables longer storage lives. It prevented oxidation of meat and other

food products, keeping them tasting and looking fresh.
Newer vacuum packing techniques replace the atmospheric
air inside packages with a protective gas mix to prevent
contact with oxygen, carbon dioxide and humidity, and to
delay microbial spoilage.

Fresh fruit and vegetables account for a large proportion
of wasted food. A certain level of humidity is needed to keep
produce from drying out, but tightly sealed packaging traps
moisture, which contributes to decomposition. The Danish
Ministry of Environment and Food launched an effort to
develop packaging that would keep fruit and vegetables
from spoiling in supermarkets. Researchers at the National
University of Singapore are experimenting with chitosan (a
polymer derived from crustacean shells) and grapefruit seeds
to create packaging for bread and other perishable foods that
will delay spoilage. Extending the viability of packaged foods
will help both shop personnel and consumers make the right
decisions about whether to keep food or throw it out.

Apeel Sciences based in Santa Barbara, California, created
a substance called 'Edipeel'. When applied to fresh produce,
it reduces decay from transpiration, oxidation and microbial
activity. This 'skin' is **completely organic** and made from
recycled agricultural products. Other companies, such as It's
Fresh in the UK, are placing filters on bananas and other fruit
and vegetables to absorb ethylene. These filters extend the life
of produce for several days.

Beyond the packaging itself, new high-tech devices are
helping keep food fresh longer. VTT, the Technical Research
Centre of Finland, has developed a sensor that detects
ethanol in food packages and transmits spoilage information

via a radio-frequency identification (RFID) tag to a mobile phone or computer. This system could help 'improve the shelf life of packaged food products, and can help better control and monitor food quality throughout the distribution chain'.[24]

Other smart packaging techniques include visual indicators that provide information about the quality of the food, its storage history and its state of freshness or deterioration. They can show the level of ripeness in fruit, for instance, and whether there have been gaps in the refrigeration of vegetables. This system is more accurate than preset 'best before' dates and gives confidence to retailers and customers that freshness or sell-by dates may not provide.

Significant progress has been made towards reducing, reusing and recycling food packaging and replacing non-biodegradable materials with compostable ones. Packaging has become 'leaner' and product shelf life has increased. Research continues into innovative packaging methods, yet vast quantities of food and beverage packaging still end up in landfills, gutters and oceans around the world. Yet another concern is that food packaging, including when it is biodegradable and compostable, may contain toxic chemicals. Short- and long-term health risks and environmental effects associated with these chemicals are unknown.

EPILOGUE

Few weeks pass without a major conference somewhere in the world focused on reducing food waste. Government agencies, non-profit organizations and for-profit businesses regularly launch new projects, initiatives and inventions intended to lessen the waste of food. Academics release new studies and make recommendations on various aspects of food waste. Thousands of organizations are engaged in rescuing good edible food from farmers, processors, retailers and other sources to help feed those in need. New facilities are funded or go into operation for the conversion of organic waste into compost or renewable energy, and innovators release new equipment or artificial intelligence technology intended to improve planning throughout the food system. Foundations and investors are pouring hundreds of millions of dollars into start-ups and projects to stop food waste.

Entrepreneurs around the world are upcycling what was once considered garbage and converting it into usable resources that can be sold for a profit. New apps and platforms are helping to reduce food waste from farm to supermarket to home kitchen. Chefs and bartenders are publishing recipes and cookbooks that show how fruit peels, vegetable seeds and other kitchen 'trash' can be transformed into delicious dishes and drinks. Cities and regional governments are launching new recycling programmes, funding new projects or restricting certain types of waste. New composting and biogas facilities are opening up in many countries.

Food-waste reduction classes and activities have been launched in pre-collegiate schools and universities, and educational programmes on the topic regularly appear on television and the Internet. Documentaries explore the issues and disseminate methods proven successful in reducing waste. Locally, nationally and internationally, government officials, environmentalists and business leaders institute new programmes and proclaim ambitious long-term goals for further improvement. It is likely that reducing, recycling and reusing food that would otherwise be thrown away will remain a top priority throughout the world for the foreseeable future.

Despite excellent progress, the war on food waste has generated only partial answers to three major questions. Question number one: how can we allow food to be wasted while so many people go hungry? As virtually all articles, books and films on the subject point out, there is more than enough food grown, raised or caught to feed everyone, yet hundreds of millions suffer from food insecurity, malnutrition or starvation. From a production standpoint, there is no explanation for this. Today, thousands of food banks and food recovery organizations operating in 57 countries are playing a key role in tackling food waste, acquiring excess edible food from farms, retailers and food-service operations and delivering it to local agencies that distribute it to those in need. Gleaners pick fruit and vegetables after the main harvest and split harvests with farmers, pickers and food recovery organizations. Supermarkets donate surplus produce and baked goods, and packaged foods nearing their expiration dates. Some supermarkets and other retail operations are required to donate edible food to food recovery organizations, and they may receive a tax deduction for doing so. In some cafeterias, students can leave packaged goods on 'share tables' for fellow students who may be hungry. Community fridges operate in cities that permit food to be placed in accessible public locations for those in need. Other communities run low-cost or 'pay-as-you-feel' grocery stores and restaurants, making it possible for those in need to get a hot meal or stock up on groceries at little or no cost.

All these programmes should be encouraged and expanded, but analysts argue that the problems of mal nutrition and hunger are highly complex and will require complex solutions. Some complain that 'charitable food aid is a sticking plaster on a gaping wound of systemic inequality in our societies'. They are opposed to 'leftover food' for "left behind" people'. They believe that existing programmes have entrenched food poverty further. They argue that new food distribution systems and anti-poverty programmes must be implemented within communities, across countries and worldwide to guarantee that no one suffers from hunger and other issues related to poverty.

As the world's population is expected to increase from 7.7 billion today to 9.1 billion by 2050, improving food distribution must be a high priority in the future. But in the meantime, food and hunger programmes are providing food for those in need and these programmes are reducing the environmental effects of surplus food ending up in landfill and mitigating an estimated 10.54 billion kg of CO_2 emissions a year.[2]

The second question is why should edible food (and food that was once edible) be dumped into landfills, where it produces methane that is a major contributor to global warming? Food that is no longer edible can be collected along with other organic waste and converted into animal feed, biogas or compost. Some local governments require businesses and residents to separate organic waste for pickup and conversion; others have launched voluntary programmes. Many new public programmes and private companies have been launched to divert food waste into animal feed, fertilizers, biofuel and power generation, and these programmes are anticipated to soar in the future. These programmes ensure that less food ends up in landfill, thus mitigating its negative effects on the environment. Anything that reduces the amount of food and other organic matter in landfill is commendable, but the food system remains a major contributor to environmental degradation via the inputs – fertilizer, pesticides, water and energy – that go into producing and transporting food that is eventually wasted.

The final question is why should a potential resource like food waste be thrown away? Perhaps the most surprising aspect of the war on food waste is the rapid rise of non-profit and for-profit companies that have improved planning for waste reduction in homes and businesses. Consulting firms help businesses improve their operating efficiency by reducing waste and recycling the waste that is unavoidable. Start-ups around the world are converting inedible food waste into useful products. New apps and packaging technology make it possible for supermarket chains to sell food closer to its 'best before' date and homemakers to consume it closer to its use-by date.

Governments, corporations and communities have announced deadlines, such as the year 2025 or 2030, for reducing waste by certain percentages. Reports are released regularly showing that businesses and consumers can save substantial amounts of money by improving their buying, transporting, storing and planning procedures. Thanks to these efforts, farmers, food producers, retailers and consumers are more aware of food waste and the need to reduce it.

The major challenge confronting the reduction of food waste is agricultural overproduction. It is in everyone's interest to maximize production: farmers, manufacturers and retailers can sell more, and consumers benefit from lower prices. Even if effective distribution systems were created around the world such that everyone had access to adequate nourishment, there would still be massive amounts of excess food produced. Converting it into animal feed, compost or other products would be preferable to tossing it into landfill or incinerating it, but better still would be not to produce it in the first place. Some overproduction will always be necessary: growers can never project how much of their crops will be lost to inclement weather, equipment breakdowns or a variety of other challenges, and a shortfall could result in malnutrition and hunger, but when food systems produce

20 to 30 per cent more food than is necessary to feed everyone, the obvious result is massive food waste.

Overproduction has lowered the cost of food, but the unintended consequence is the ease with which food is discarded all along the supply chain, from producers to retailers to consumers. An over-abundance of affordable food also contributes to overeating and obesity, which plague people in industrialized countries. Food-waste projects and programmes have helped ameliorate the problems of excess production, but better systemic planning is necessary to reduce production if food waste is to be significantly reduced.

Initiatives reducing waste won't solve all the problems of the global food system, but they are a beginning. Unlike many other issues related to food systems, food waste is one that each of us can understand and to which each of us can make positive contributions. This offers cautious optimism for the future.

REFERENCES

1 WAR ON FOOD WASTE

1 World Economic Forum, www.weforum.org, 6 May 2019.
2 Rebecca Smithers, 'Instagram Generation Is Fuelling UK Food Waste Mountain, Study Finds', *The Guardian*, 10 February 2017.
3 R. W. Wenlock et al., 'Household Food Wastage in Britain', *British Journal of Nutrition*, XLIII (January 1980), pp. 53–70.
4 USDA, 'Nutrient Content of the U.S. Food Supply, 1909–2010', www.cnpp.usda.gov, 2 May 2019.
5 Mike Schiller, 'Waste Land: Does the Large Amount of Food Discarded in the U.S. Take a Toll on the Environment?', *Scientific American*, www.scientificamerican.com, 2 May 2019.
6 European Commission, 'Council Directive 1999/31/EC', 26 April 1999.
7 'The End of Cheap Food', *The Economist*, 6 December 2007.
8 James Chapman, 'As Supermarket Prices Spiral Brown Tells Families: "Stop Wasting Food"', *Daily Mail*, 7 July 2008.
9 C. Nellemann et al., eds, *The Environmental Food Crisis: The Environment's Role in Averting Future Food Crises: A UNEP Rapid Response Assessment*, Arendal, Norway: United Nations Environment Programme, February 2009.
10 Jonathan Bloom, 'Denmark Capitalizes on Culture to Stop Food Waste', *The Plate*, www.nationalgeographic.com, 26 September 2016.
11 Dominic Hogg et al., *Dealing with Food Waste in the UK*, report prepared for WRAP by Eunomia Research and Consulting, Bristol, March 2007.
12 Waste and Resources Action Programme, *The Food We Waste*, Food Waste Report, Banbury, UK, May 2008.
13 Rachel Shields, 'Kitchen Bin War: Tackling the Food Waste

Mountain', *The Independent*, www.independent.co.uk, 7 June 2009.

14 Gabriel Borrud, 'Germany Launches Initiative to Reduce Food Waste', Made for Minds, www.dw.com, 13 March 2012.

2 FARMED WASTE

1 Sandrine Badio, 'Understanding Gleaning: Historical and Cultural Contexts of the Shift from Rural to Urban Models for the Improvement of Food Security', Senior Honours Thesis, Lakehead University, Thunder Bay, Ontario (2009).

2 Bruno Waterfield, 'EU to Allow Sale of "Odd" Shaped Fruit and Vegetables', *The Telegraph*, www.telegraph.co.uk, 12 November 2008; Rebecca Smithers, 'Jamie Oliver Leads Drive to Buy Misshapen Fruit and Vegetables', *The Guardian*, www.theguardian.com, 1 January 2015.

3 'Left-out: An Investigation of Fruit and Vegetable Losses on the Farm', Natural Resources Defense Council, December 2012, p. 3.

4 'Farmers Talk Food Waste: Supermarkets' Role in Crop Waste on UK Farms', *Feedback Global*, February 2018, available at https://feedbackglobal.org.

5 T. M. Bond et al., *Food Waste within Global Food Systems: A Global Food Security Report*, Global Food Security Programme (Swindon, 2013).

6 Suzanne Goldenberg, 'Half of All U.S. Food Produce Is Thrown Away, New Research Suggests', *The Guardian*, 13 September 2016.

7 Smithers, 'Jamie Oliver Leads Drive to Buy Misshapen Fruit and Vegetables'.

8 Jenny Splitter, 'How Hungry Harvest Uses Technology to Combat Food Waste', *Forbes*, www.forbes.com, 31 October 2018.

9 Rubies in the Rubble, www.rubiesintherubble.com

10 'Trending: Local Solutions Could Hold the Key to Reducing Global Food Waste', *Sustainable Brands*, https://sustainablebrands.com, 5 January 2018.

11 Michael Gove, 'Oxford Farming Conference 2019 Address by the Environment Secretary', www.gov.uk, 3 January 2019.

3 MANUFACTURED WASTE

1 Manoj Dora et al., 'Importance of Sustainable Operations in Food Loss: Evidence from the Belgian Food Processing Industry', *Annals of Operations Research*, CCLXXV/17 (January 2019).
2 Erin McCormick, 'Recalls of "Potentially Lethal" U.S. Meat and Poultry Nearly Double since 2013', *The Guardian*, www.theguardian.com, 18 January 2019.
3 Jessi Devenyns, 'From Trash to Treasure: Upcycled Food Waste Is Worth $46.7b', Food Dive, www.fooddive.com, 22 May 2019.
4 Craig Hanson and Peter Mitchell, *The Business Case for Reducing Food Loss and Waste: A Report on Behalf of Champions 12.3*, Champions 12.3, March 2017, available at https://champions123.org.
5 PB&J = 'Peanut Butter and Jelly', historically associated with a sandwich that children enjoyed.
6 Technik Packing Services, 'The History of Expiration Dates on Food and Consumables Packaging', Technik Packing Services, n.d.
7 Rose Eveleth, '"Sell By", and "Best By" Dates on Food Are Basically Made Up – But Hard to Get Rid Of; Where Do These Dates Even Come From, and Why Do We Have Them?', Smithsonian.com, 28 March 2014.
8 Rachel Shields, 'Kitchen Bin War: Tackling the Food Waste Mountain', *The Independent*, www.independent.co.uk, 6 June 2009.
9 Emily Broad Leib et al., 'The Dating Game: How Confusing Food Date Labels Lead to Food Waste in America', New York, the Natural Resources Defense Council, The Harvard Food Law and Policy Clinic (Cambridge, MA, September 2013).
10 'India Pilot Study Shows How the Cold Chain Can Help Reduce Food Loss and Carbon Emissions', *Carrier*, 2 December 2016.
11 World Economic Forum, 'Innovation with a Purpose: Improving Traceability in Food Value Chains through Technology Innovations' (Cologny and Geneva, January 2020), p. 10.

4 SUPERMARKET WASTE

1 Joan Gross, 'Capitalism and Its Discontents: Back-to-the-lander and Freegan Foodways in Rural Oregon', in *Taking Food Public:*

Redefining Foodways in a Changing World, ed. P. Williams-Forson and C. Counihan (New York, 2012), p. 79.

2 Joan Gross, '"Freegans" and Foragers Form New Foodways', *OSU Newsletter* (Spring 2008).

3 John Preston, 'Waste: Uncovering the Global Food Scandal by Tristram Stuart: Review', *The Telegraph*, www.telegraph.co.uk, 12 July 2009.

4 'Stop Wasting Food, Brown Urging', BBC News, www.bbc.co.uk/news, 7 July 2008.

5 Dominic Lawson, 'I'm Sorry, but Brown Is Talking Rubbish', *The Independent*, www.independent.co.uk, 8 July 2008.

6 Tristram Stuart, 'Post-harvest Losses: A Neglected Field', in *State of the World 2011: Innovations That Nourish the Planet: A Worldwatch Institute Report on Progress toward a Sustainable Society*, ed. Danielle Nierenberg and Brian Halweil (New York, 2011), chap. 9, pp. 99–100.

7 Erica Johnson, 'Walmart Insider Says "Heartbreaking" Amount of Food Dumped in Trash', CBC News, www.cbc.ca, 24 October 2016.

8 Melissa Mancini et al., 'Walmart Says It Has Reduced Food Waste by 20% since CBC Investigation', CBC News, www.cbc.ca, 27 October 2017.

9 Katharine Schmidt, 'The Road to Ending Food Waste', *Huffington Post*, www.huffingtonpost.ca, 29 November 2016.

10 FoodCloud, www.food.cloud, accessed 8 May 2019.

11 Daily Table, www.dailytable.org, accessed 6 May 2019.

12 Hazel Sheffield, 'The UK's First Food Waste Supermarket Opens', *The Independent*, www.independent.co.uk, 20 September 2016.

13 The Courtauld Commitment 2025, see www.wrap.org.uk/content/what-is-courtauld.

14 David Cohen, 'Food for London: Sadiq Khan and Sainsbury's Support Our Campaign on Food Waste', *Evening Standard*, https://news.sky.com, 22 September 2016.

15 'Food Waste: UK's Major Supermarkets Sign up to Halve £20bn Annual Bill by 2030', *Sky News*, https://news.sky.com, 13 June 2019.

16 Craig Hanson, '2030 Champions Brings Together Business and Government to Cut U.S. Food Waste', World Resources Institute, 17 November 2016.

5 RESTAURANT WASTE

1 'Food Waste: Tier 1 Assessment Prepared for GMA/FMI', Grocery Manufacturers Association (GMA) and Food Marketing Institute (FMI), March 2012.

2 Food Waste Alliance, 'Analysis of U.S. Food Waste among Food Manufacturers, Retailers, and Restaurants', www.foodwastealliance.org.

3 Dana Gunders, 'Wasted: How America Is Losing Up to 40 Percent of Its Food from Farm to Fork to Landfill' (Research Report No. 12-06-B), Natural Resources Defense Council, August 2012.

4 Austin Cowles et al., 'The Business Case for Reducing Food Loss and Waste: Restaurants', Champions 12.3, 14 February 2019, available at https://champions123.org.

5 Theresa Ehrlich, '6 Ways Restaurants Can Fight Food Waste', EDF+Business – Environmental Defense Fund, business.edf.org, 14 March 2017.

6 Aurelien Breeden, 'Brushing off a French Stigma That Doggie Bags Are for Beggars', *New York Times*, www.nytimes.com, 14 November 2014.

7 'National Restaurant Association Conserve Hosts Free Webinars on How "Going Green" Can Improve the Bottom Line', National Restaurant Association, 17 September 2008.

8 Morgane Nyfeler and Poppy Roy, 'Vogue's Guide to the Best Zero-waste Restaurants', *Vogue*, www.vogue.co.uk, 18 October 2018.

9 Alex Renton, 'Food Waste Solutions: Cuttlefish Testicles and Pigs' Blood', *The Guardian*, www.theguardian.com, 6 February 2014.

10 Shanaka Fernando and Greg Ronald Hill, *Lentil as Anything: Everybody Deserves a Place at the Table* (Fremantle, Western Australia, 2012).

11 'Tech co Winnow, Sustainability co Diversey Team up to Fight Food Waste', FNBnews, www.fnbnews.com, 26 December 2017.

12 Oliver Moore, 'Schnippeldisko: The Disco That Fights Food Waste!', Agricultural and Rural Convention, www.arc2020.eu, 20 January 2014.

13 Laura Price, 'Why Massimo Bottura Wants the World to View Food Waste as Viable Ingredients', The World's 50 Best Restaurants, www.theworlds50best.com, 7 June 2017.

6 CONSUMER WASTE

1 Dave C. Lovea et al., 'Wasted Seafood in the United States: Quantifying Loss from Production to Consumption and Moving toward Solutions', *Global Environmental Change*, xxxv (November 2015), pp. 116–24.

2 'u.s. Set to Get a Whole Lot Smarter at ces 2017', Smarter press release, https://smarter.am, 3 January 2017; Lucy Cormack, 'Food Waste Averages $3800 per Household, Yet Food Insecurity at "Crisis" Point', *Sydney Morning Herald*, www.smh.com.au, 3 June 2017.

3 Tom Jackson, 'Could Tech Reduce Food Waste and Help Feed the World?', bbc News, www.bbc.co.uk/news, 17 June 2016.

4 Susan Edmunds, 'Food Waste Costs New Zealand $870m', *Stuff*, www.stuff.co.nz, 6 November 2015.

5 'Herald View: The Waste of Money That Should Put All to Shame', *Herald Scotland*, www.heraldscotland.com, 19 November 2016.

6 Arutz Sheva Staff, 'Report: Israelis Threw out 2.5 Million Tons of Food Last Year', *Israel National News*, www.israelnationalnews.com, 3 March 2019.

7 Sylvia Thompson, 'Turning Food Waste into Profit', *Irish Times*, www.irishtimes.com, 3 June 2017.

8 Eddie Yoon, 'The Grocery Industry Confronts a New Problem: Only 10% of Americans Love Cooking', *Harvard Business Review*, https://hbr.org, 22 September 2017.

9 Mary Griffin et al., 'An Analysis of a Community Food Waste Stream', *Agriculture and Human Values*, xxvi (March 2009), pp. 67–81.

10 Brent R. Heard et al., 'Comparison of Life Cycle Environmental Impacts from Meal Kits and Grocery Store Meals', *Resources, Conservation and Recycling*, 23 April 2019, available at css.umich.edu.

11 'This Restaurant Is Making Nutritious Veggie Burgers from Leftover Juice Pulp!', Food Monster app, 8 December 2017.

12 Brennan Hogan, 'Technology Trumps Food Waste in South Korea', LeanPath, https://blog.leanpath.com, 29 May 2015; Max S. Kim, 'The Country Winning the Battle on Food Waste', *HuffPost*, www.huffingtonpost.co.uk, 8 April 2019.

13 Katie Morley, 'Shoppers Face Food Waste Warnings in Supermarkets, as Levels Rise for the First Time in a Decade', *The Telegraph*, www.telegraph.co.uk, 10 January 2017.

14 Danyi Qi and Brian E. Roe, 'Household Food Waste: Multivariate Regression and Principal Components Analyses of Awareness and Attitudes among U.S. Consumers', *PLOS ONE*, 21 July 2016.

15 'New Zealand Food Waste Research Love Food Hate Waste Campaign Evaluation 2018', Love Food Hate Waste, www.lovefoodhatewaste.co.nz, accessed 5 March 2020.

16 Sligo County Council, 'Final Report: National Brown Bin Awareness Pilot Scheme in Sligo City', Riverside, Sligo, Ireland, 1 February 2019.

7 FOOD-RELATED WASTE

1 Kenneth Marsh and Betty Bugusu, 'Food Packaging – Roles, Materials, and Environmental Issues', *Journal of Food Science*, vxxii (April 2007), pp. R39–R55.

2 Center for Biological Diversity, 'Ocean Plastics Pollution: A Global Tragedy for Our Oceans and Sea Life', www.biologicaldiversity.org, accessed 10 February 2020.

3 The National Academies Press, 'Review of the Styrene Assessment in the National Toxicology Program 12th Report on Carcinogens' (2014), p. 383.

4 Rebecca Rupp, 'France Just Banned Plastic Forks. What's Next?', *National Geographic*, www.nationalgeographic.com, 3 November 2016.

5 Petcore Europe, www.petcore-europe.org, 2 May 2019.

6 Office fédéral de l'environnement OFEV, '93% de tous les emballages pour boissons sont recyclés', 3 September 2013.

7 Ellen Gamerman, 'An Inconvenient Bag', *Wall Street Journal*, www.wsj.com, 26 September 2008; 'Zimbabwe Bans Plastic Foam Containers to Protect Environment', VOA News, www.voanws.com, 14 July 2017.

8 Adam Minter, 'How a Ban on Plastic Bags Can Go Wrong', BloombergView, www.bloombergview.com, 18 August 2015.

9 Rupp, 'France Just Banned Plastic Forks'.

10 Abha Bhattarai, 'Paper, Bamboo, Twizzlers: Restaurants Consider Alternatives to the Plastic Straw', *Washington Post*, www.washingtonpost.com, 2 February 2018.

11 'Are Straw Pledges Bending the Truth?', *Footprint*, www.foodservicefootprint.com, 4 February 2018.

12 Charlie Heller, 'Could the UK Bring an End to Paper Coffee Cups?', *Food and Wine*, www.foodandwine.com, 5 January 2018.

13 Inna Lazareva, 'Coffee-fuelled Buses to Disco Soups: Five Quirky Uses of Waste in 2017', *Reuters*, news.trust.org, 22 December 2017.

14 Sian Sutherland, 'UK Supermarkets Must Take Lead in Tackling Plastic Pollution', *Earth Times*, www.earthtimes.org, 1 June 2017.

15 Marcus Eriksen et al., 'Plastic Pollution in the World's Oceans: More Than 5 Trillion Plastic Pieces Weighing Over 250,000 Tons Afloat at Sea', *PLOS ONE*, 10 December 2014.

16 Alister Doyle, 'Plastic Found in Mussels from Arctic to China – Enters Human Food', *Reuters*, 20 December 2017.

17 American Chemical Society, 'Cutting Food Waste, But Tossing More Packaging: Our Plastics Conundrum', American Chemical Society, www.acs.org, 19 October 2016.

18 Benjamin Senaur et al., *Food Trends and the Changing Consumer* (St Paul, MN, 1991), p. 289.

19 'Courtauld Commitment 3 Delivers over £100 Million Business Savings by Reducing Food Waste over Three Year Period', WRAP, www.wrap.org.uk, 10 January 2017.

20 Sustainable Brands, 'Trending: Food Waste Inspires Visionary Kitchen, New Packaging; Human Waste Inspires . . . Beer?', www.sustainablebrands.com, 5 August 2016.

21 Cody Boteler, 'Study: Increase Packaging, Reduce Food Waste', *Waste Dive*, www.wastedive.com, 24 January 2018; Kyle Fisher et al., 'Quantifying the Value of Packaging as a Strategy to Prevent Food Waste in America', Ameripen, January 2018.

22 Piotr Barczak, 'Why Single-use Packaging Will Preserve Europe's Food Waste Problem', *Resource Magazine*, 8 September 2016.

23 Delia Paul, 'UNEA-4 Commits to Global Environmental Data Strategy, Reducing Single-use Plastics', SDG Knowledge Hub, 19 March 2019.

24 Olli Ernvall, 'Sensor Detects Spoilage of Food', Phys.org, 6 May 2015.

EPILOGUE

1 Olivier de Schutter et al., 'Food Banks Are No Solution to Poverty', *The Guardian*, www.theguardian.com, 24 March 2019.
2 Doug O'Brien et al., 'Waste Not, Want Not – Toward Zero Hunger: Food Banks – A Green Solution to Hunger', The Global FoodBanking Network (2019), www.foodbanking.org, accessed 18 December 2019.

FOOD WASTE RESOURCES

GENERAL BOOKS

Baglioni, Simone, et al., eds, *Foodsaving in Europe: At the Crossroad of Social Innovation* (Cham, Switzerland, 2017)

Bloom, Jonathan, *American Wasteland: How America Throws Away Nearly Half of Its Food (And What We Can Do About It)* (Cambridge, MA, 2010)

Evans, David, *Food Waste: Home Consumption, Material Culture and Everyday Life* (New York, 2014)

—, Hugh Campbell and Anne Murcott, *Waste Matters: New Perspectives on Food and Society* (Hoboken, NJ, 2013)

Fernando, Shanaka, and Greg Ronald Hill, *Lentil as Anything: Everybody Deserves a Place at the Table* (Fremantle, WA, 2012)

Galanakis, Charis Michael, *Saving Food: Production, Supply Chain, Food Waste and Food Consumption* (Waltham, MA, 2019)

Gunjal, Aparna B., *Global Initiatives for Waste Reduction and Cutting Food Loss* (Hershey, PA, 2019)

Kosseva, Maria R., and Colin Webb, eds, *Food Industry Wastes: Assessment and Recuperation of Commodities* (Waltham, MA, 2013)

Naraine, Leighton, *Optimizing the Use of Farm Waste and Non-farm Waste to Increase Productivity and Food Security: Emerging Research and Opportunities* (Hershey, PA, 2019)

Poltronieri, Palmiro, and Oscar Fernando D'Urso, eds, *Biotransformation of Agricultural Waste and By-products: The Food, Feed, Fibre, Fuel (4F) Economy* (Amsterdam, 2016)

Segrè, Andrea, and Silvia Gaiani, *Transforming Food Waste into a Resource* (Cambridge, 2011)

Stuart, Tristram, *Waste: Uncovering the Global Food Scandal*
　　(New York, 2009)
Yahia, Elhadi, ed., *Preventing Food Losses and Waste to Achieve Food
　　Security and Sustainability* (Cambridge, 2019)

DUMPSTER DIVING AND FREEGANISM

Barnard, Alex V., *Freegans: Diving into the Wealth of Food Waste
　　in America* (Minneapolis, MN, 2016)
Ferrell, Jeff, *Empire of Scrounge: Inside the Urban Underground of
　　Dumpster Diving, Trash Picking, and Street Scavenging* (New
　　York, 2005)
Greenfield, Rob, *Dude Making a Difference: Bamboo Bikes, Dumpster
　　Dives and Other Extreme Adventures across America* (Gabriola
　　Island, BC, 2015)

COOKBOOKS

Bloomfield, April, *A Girl and Her Greens: Hearty Meals from the
　　Garden* (New York, 2015)
——, *A Girl and Her Pig: Recipes and Stories* (New York, 2012)
Bottura, Massimo, *Bread Is Gold: Extraordinary Meals with Ordinary
　　Ingredients* (London, 2017)
Bowler, Suzy, *Creative Ways to Use Up Leftovers: An Inspiring A–Z
　　of Ingredients and Delicious Ideas* (London, 2018)
Duggan, Tara, *Root-to-Stalk Cooking: The Art of Using the Whole
　　Vegetable* (New York, 2013)
Elliott-Howery, Alex, and Sabine Spindler, *Cornersmith: Salads and
　　Pickles: Vegetables with More Taste and Less Waste* (Sydney, 2019)
Fearnley-Whittingstall, Hugh, Simon de Courcy Wheeler and Tim
　　Hopgood, *River Cottage Love Your Leftovers: Recipes for the
　　Resourceful Cook* (London, 2015)
Gamoran, Joe, *Cooking Scrappy: 100 Recipes to Help You Stop Wasting
　　Food, Save Money, and Love What You Eat* (New York, 2018)
Glass, Victoria, *Too Good to Waste: How to Eat Everything* (London, 2017)
Gunders, Dana, *Waste-free Kitchen Handbook: A Guide to Eating Well
　　and Saving Money by Wasting Less Food* (San Francisco, CA, 2015)
Hard, Lindsay-Jean, *Cooking with Scraps: Turn Your Peels, Cores,
　　Rinds, and Stems into Delicious Meals* (New York, 2018)

Henderson, Fergus, *Beyond Nose to Tail: More Omnivorous Recipes for the Adventurous Cook* (New York, 2008)

——, *The Complete Nose to Tail: A Kind of British Cooking* (London, 2012)

——, *Nose to Tail Eating: A Kind of British Cooking* (London, 1999)

Juul, Selina, et al., *Stop spild af mad: en kogebog med mere* (Copenhagen, 2011)

Love, Michael, Robert Irvine and Lynn Parks, *The Salvage Chef Cookbook: More than 125 Recipes, Tips, and Secrets to Transform What You Have in Your Kitchen into Delicious Dishes for the Ones You Love* (New York, 2014)

Love Food Hate Waste, *Easy Choice – Family Kai: Autumn Recipes* (Auckland, 2018)

Monaghan, Keirnan, and Theo Vamvounakis, *Waste Not: Recipes and Tips for Full-use Cooking from America's Best Chefs* (New York, 2018)

Refslund, Mads, and Tama Matsuoka Wong, *Scraps, Wilt and Weeds: Turning Wasted Food into Plenty* (New York, 2017)

Satterfield, Steven, *Root to Leaf: A Southern Chef Cooks through the Seasons* (New York, 2015)

Stone, Matt, *The Natural Cook: Maximum Taste, Zero Waste* (Crows Nest, nsw, 2016)

Woods, Rich, *The Cocktail Guy: Infusions, Distillations and Innovative Combinations* (London, 2017)

FILMS AND DOCUMENTARIES

Dive! (dir. Jeremy Seifert, 2009), www.divethefilm.com

Expired? Food Waste in America (dir. Emily Broad Leib and Nathaniel Hansen, 2016), www.notreallyexpired.com

Food Fighter (dir. Daniel Goldberg, 2018), starring Ronni Kahn, www.foodfighterfilm.com

Global Waste: The Scandal of Food Waste (dir. Olivier Lemaire, 2011), starring Tristram Stuart, www.newendistribution.com

Just Eat It: A Food Waste Movie (dir. Grant and Jen Baldwin, 2015), starring Jonathan Bloom, Tristram Stuart and Dana Gunders, www.foodwastemovie.com

Wasted! The Story of Food Waste (dir. Anna Chai and Nari Kye, 2017), starring Anthony Bourdain, Dan Barber, Mario Batali, Danny Bowien and Massimo Bottura, www.wastedfilm.com

ORGANIZATIONS

Banki Żywności (Poland), www.bankizywnosci.pl
Caritas (Vatican City), www.caritas.org
Champions 12.3 (Global), www.champions123.org
Disco Soup (France), www.discosoupe.org
EndFoodWaste (U.S.), www.endfoodwaste.org
Feedback Global (London-based), www.feedbackglobal.org
Feeding the 5000 (UK-based), www.feedbackglobal.org/campaigns/
    feeding-the-5000
Feeding America (Chicago-based), www.feedingamerica.org
Fondazione Banco Alimentare Onlus (Italy),
    www.bancoalimentare.it
Food for Soul (Modena, Italy), www.foodforsoul.it
Food Tank: The Think Tank for Food (New Orleans-based),
    www.foodtank.com
Food Waste Fiasco (U.S.), www.robgreenfield.tv
FoodForward SA (South Africa), www.foodforwardsa.org
FoodSharing.de (Germany), www.foodsharing.de
Gleaning Network EU, www.feedbackglobal.org/
    gleaning-network-eu-2
Gleaning Network UK, www.feedbackglobal.org/campaigns/
    gleaning-network
The Global FoodBanking Network (U.S.-based), www.foodbanking.
    org
Harvard Food Law and Policy Clinic (Cambridge, MA),
    www.hls.harvard.edu
Last Minute Market (Bologna, Italy), www.lastminutemarket.it
Love Food Hate Waste (Australia), www.lovefoodhatewaste.com
Natural Resources Defense Council (U.S.-based), www.nrdc.org
OzHarvest (Australia), www.ozharvest.org
ReFood (UK), www.refood.co.uk
Resource Efficient Food and dRink for Entire Supply cHain
    [*sic*] – REFRESH – (Wageningen, Netherlands-based),
    www.eu-refresh.org
Les Restos du Coeur (France), www.restosducoeur.org
Stop Wasting Food – Stop Spild Af Mad (Copenhagen, Denmark),
    www.stopwastingfoodmovement.org
The Real Junk Food Project (UK) www.trjfp.com

United Against Food Waste (Netherlands),
     www.unitedagainstfoodwaste.com
Waste and Resources Action Programme (Banbury, UK),
     www.wrap.org.uk
wastED [*sic*] (New York and London), www.wastedlondon.com
We Save Food! Wir retten Lebensmittel! (Bavaria, Germany),
     www.stmelf.bayern.de/wir-retten-lebensmittel
World Resources Institute (Washington, DC-based), www.wri.org
World Wildlife Fund (U.S.-based), www.worldwildlife.org/initiatives/
     food-waste

APPS AND PLATFORMS

BlueCart (U.S.), www.bluecart.com
BuffetGO (Finland/Scandinavia), www.buffet-go.com
Cheetah (West Africa), www.cheetah.ujuizi.com
ChowMatch (California-based), www.chowmatch.org
CropMobster (U.S.), www.cropmobster.com
Flashfood (Toronto, Canada), www.flashfood.com
FoodCloud (Ireland and UK), www.food.cloud
Food Cowboy (U.S.), www.foodcowboy.com
Food Rescue U.S. (Fairfield, CT-based), www.foodrescue.us
Food Savior (Hong Kong), www.facebook.com/foodsavior
Froodly (Helsinki, Finland), www.froodly.com
Grub Cycle (Malaysia), www.grubcycle.my/grub-bites
Karma (Sweden), www.karma.life
MintScraps (Washington, DC), www.mintscraps.com
MyFoody (Milan, Italy), www.linkedin.com/company/myfoody
Sharebite (New York), www.sharebite.com
treatsure [*sic*] (Singapore), www.treatsure.co

INDEX